Praise for *Like A Hammer*: Poets on Mass Incarceration

"*Like a Hammer* is an abundance—of brilliance, of wisdom, of compassion, of joy as an antidote for pain, and hope that beats back despair. These poems cast light into the dark corners of the carceral state, which is also to say, they illuminate our shared fortune. For fact, it comprises essential work on the failed promise of America's justice system, no less than a crucial critique of the American dream."
—Mitchell S. Jackson, author of *Survival Math: Notes on an All-American Family*

"Poets know how to make language sing and ache in the face of a brutal subject. With nuance and rhythm, these poets take up the mantle of modern blues singers, witnessing America's incarceration problem—tangled with so many other systemic oppressions—with heart and soul. Poetry is at its best here, opening questions, making us feel it in the gut, and asking us to open our eyes wider and wider. Thank you, poets, for making the statistics into human emotion so beautiful, so painfully."
—Caits Meissner, editor of *The Sentences That Create Us*

"If reading stories about incarceration is uncomfortable, imagine what it must be like to live them. How do we reconcile the harm we decry with the harm we allow? What do we owe, as a society, to the human beings—loved ones, including mine—we lock up? The work that Diana Marie Delgado has curated deftly demands that we pay, at least, attention. Indeed, how can we say we forget them, when we indulge in watching crime dramas on television that glorify law enforcers who hunt and murder with impunity, as incarcerators quietly profit from entrapment, bloodshed, and the grief of shattered families?

I write this endorsement as someone who experienced the fallout from outside, who witnessed the all-encompassing impact of prison time on family, friends, and community members. What gets glossed over as a source of shame and street cred flattens the dynamic silences that shape tired public discourses—habits of speech and thought this anthology disrupts, challenging unevolved views of crime and punishment and exposing them as a shabby illusion of protection.

Poetry offers us a distilled source of emotional reportage—the kind of knowledge we need if we are ever to evolve to higher levels of humanity. From the machines and tortures invented to interrogate humans, to the landscapes and buildings designed to keep incarceration a sinister echo in the mind, to the tactics and tricks used to extinguish even the thought of escape from either arrest or a sentence, the poems in this anthology unveil the ugly totality of imprisonment now and throughout history. *Like A Hammer* gathers voices we must uplift, and in so doing, uplift ourselves."
—Khadijah Queen, author of *Anodyne* and *Radical Poetics: Essays on Literature & Culture*

LIKE A HAMMER

POETS ON MASS INCARCERATION

Edited by Diana Marie Delgado

Foreword by Keeanga-Yamahtta Taylor

Haymarket Books
Chicago, Illinois

© 2025 Diana Marie Delgado

Published in 2025 by
Haymarket Books
P.O. Box 180165
Chicago, IL 60618
773-583-7884
www.haymarketbooks.org
info@haymarketbooks.org

ISBN: 979-8-88890-247-9

Distributed to the trade in the US through Consortium Book Sales and Distribution (www.cbsd.com) and internationally through Ingram Publisher Services International (www.ingramcontent.com).

This book was published with the generous support of Lannan Foundation, Wallace Action Fund, and the Marguerite Casey Foundation.

Special discounts are available for bulk purchases by organizations and institutions. Please email info@haymarketbooks.org for more information.

Cover design by Rachel Cohen.

Printed in Canada by union labor.

Library of Congress Cataloging-in-Publication data is available.

10 9 8 7 6 5 4 3 2 1

Contents

FOREWORD: THE ARMY OF THE WRONGED ... XI
INTRODUCTION ... I

I. Time Rules This Empire: Where Clocks Stand Still

Randall Horton
  : .Or. This *Malus* Thing Never to Be Confused with Justice ... 9

Hanif Abdurraqib
  All the TV Shows Are about Cops ... 10

Sin à Tes Souhaits
  TRAP noun. \'trap\ ... 12

Rhionna Anderson
  Marriage ... 14

Christopher Malec
  Which Is It? ... 15

Vanessa Angélica Villarreal
  Architect 1 ... 16

Reginald Dwayne Betts
  Blood History ... 23

Sandra Jackson
  Lost ... 24

Natalie Diaz
  Under Correction I ... 25

Christina Pernini
  Behind the Wall ... 27

II. Be Careful How You Speak about Rainbows: Beauty & Grace

Eduardo Martinez
   A.G.A.M.   31

Catherine LaFleur
   Bloom   36

Marcelo Hernandez Castillo
   Eclogue: A Field Guide and Cure   37

Kennedy A. Gisege
   Scattered Like Yellow Feathers   43

Roque Raquel Salas Rivera
   En las primeras décadas del nuevo siglo   44

Roque Raquel Salas Rivera
   In the First Decades of the New Century   46

Tongo Eisen-Martin
   Knees Next to Their Wallets   48

Erica "Ewok" Walker
   D.O.C. "department of castration"   51

III. The Bill Is Past Due: The Hustle

Sin à Tes Souhaits
   10 Toes Down   55

Leeann Parker
   If I Were a Boy   56

John Murillo
   The Ballad of Stagolee, or Variation on a Theme by Sterling A. Brown with a Slight Nod to Etheridge Knight   57

Brian Batchelor
   Political Arithmetic   67

Candace Williams
   black, body   69

Hanif Abdurraqib
  All the TV Shows Are about Cops   72
Kenneth Nadeau
  Everything I Know about Horses   74

IV. American Inferno: Inside the Cell

Leeann Parker
  Free   79
Evie Shockley
  american inferno   80
Christopher Malec
  Order's Up   81
Randall Horton
  Flashback to the Cell   83
Catherine LaFleur
  Devour   84
SHE > i
  Cellfish   85
Kennedy A. Gisege
  Break from Madness   86
Eduardo Martinez
  Cinderblock Calendars   87
Natalie Diaz
  Under Correction II   89
Patricia Smith
  Only One Clock   92

V. What Is Caged Is Also Kept from Us: The People

Vicki Hicks
  The First Day   99

Patricia Smith
    But the Phone Rings Sometimes   100

Ada Limón
    What Is Caged Is Also Kept from Us   104

Reginald Dwayne Betts
    When Every Word Is a Name   105

Jessica Hill
    Reasons   107

Sin à Tes Souhaits
    Sometimes I Wonder If God Really Fuck with Me Like That   108

Evie Shockley
    can't unsee   109

Cody Bruce
    Identity of a Prisoner   113

James Pearl
    My Father the Sahib   114

Gustavo Guerra
    Vacillating   115

Sarah Lynn Maatsch
    Click!   116

Angel Nafis
    Ghazal to Open Cages   117

VI. The Nakedness Dark Demands: Surveillance and Shapeshifting

Vanessa Angélica Villarreal
    Architect 3   121

Patrick Rosal
    An excerpt from "Notes from the Visitations," a work in progress   127

Nicole Sealey
   Pages Thirteen to Twenty-One from "The Ferguson
   Report: An Erasure"   136

Marina Bueno
   Brutality   153

Natalie Diaz
   Under Correction III   154

Marcelo Hernandez Castillo
   Sonnet Triptych   158

Roque Raquel Salas Rivera
   La promiscuidad tan indeseable   163

Roque Raquel Salas Rivera
   Such Undesirable Promiscuity   166

VII. Like a Hammer: The Forgotten Impoverished

Nikky Finney
   Black Boy with Cow: A Still Life   171

READING AND DISCUSSION GUIDE   189
ACKNOWLEDGMENTS   191
CONTRIBUTORS   193
GRATITUDE   199

FOREWORD: THE ARMY OF THE WRONGED

Keeanga-Yamahtta Taylor

> *What turns me cold in all this experience, is the certainty that thousands of innocent victims are in jail today because they had neither money nor friends to help them. . . . We protect and defend sensational cases where Negroes are involved. But the great mass of arrested or accused Black folk have no defense. There is a desperate need of nationwide organization to oppose this national racket of railroading to jail and chain gangs the poor, friendless and Black.*
>
> W. E. B. DuBois, 1951

In the late nineteen eighties I and a group of my junior high school classmates crammed into a small passenger van and took a three-hour ride south of Dallas to Huntsville, Texas, home of Texas's death row. We laughed as kids are prone to do, either to distract from discomfort or an aversion to thinking about what we were doing or where we were headed to. The jokes quieted to a queasy curiosity when we pulled up to the overwhelming presence of the huge state prison. We were a group of wayward barely teenagers being initiated into a program called Scared Straight. The point was to take us to prison where guards would yell at us as if we were inmates. Where inmates would ogle and say harassing things to us as we passed through the corridors. And where other prisoners serving life sentences would tell us the horrors of prison in hopes of scaring us straight.

What I remember most is that the prison was loud, almost cavernous in the way that sound echoed and bounced around the walls. There were the loud sounds of metal doors sliding into the grooves that indicated the bars were locked, the essence of the prison. We walked through several corridors where, it is clear to me now, the men had been encouraged to say hostile and menacing things to us as we passed through on our way to a classroom. I was one of two girls in the group, but most of the comments were directed at the boys, almost all sexual in nature.

When we got to the classroom, everyone sat down and resumed their nervous laughter and quiet banter. Soon thereafter, a guard arrived with two inmates who stood at the front of the classroom. When two of the boys sitting in the front row continued to talk even after the guard had told us to be quiet, one of the inmates rushed over to one of the boys, grabbed him by the shirt, and pulled him up and out of his seat. He said in the angriest voice that he could muster that he could do anything to any of us "because I am already dead." He let go of the boy, and none of us said another word unless spoken to for the rest of the day. The inmate later explained that he was serving a life sentence and he wanted to share his experiences to keep us out of the prison. Most of their presentation involved stories about how they ended up in Huntsville and the misery of life in prison. They talked about the violence of prison, including rape and sexual assault. The men made sure to tell me and the other girl that if we ended up in a woman's prison that we would not be safe from rape as he told stories about women being raped by other women.

After a morning of stories about the violence and misery of the prison, we had lunch in the cafeteria surrounded by inmates and guards. The guards explained that they ate the same hot lunch that the inmates consumed to make sure they were not putting glass or other substances in the food. We stood in line and were served smothered pork chops and rice, and then we ate with guards and prisoners. At least three inmates approached me and told me they were innocent. By the end of the day, when we drove back to Dallas, it was completely silent, unlike the drive down. The entire experience was surreal and something about it was effective for me, at least. I had been scared straight out of something, I was not quite sure, but I knew that this was the last time I ever wanted to see the inside of a prison.

Thinking back on that experience, I realize how degrading it was. At the core of the program was the goal to convince us that the imprisoned were monsters deserving of whatever brutality and violence they encountered in the prison. The program accepted the untamed brutality and the deplorable condition of the prison as an acceptable and appropriate punishment for whatever crimes had landed the unfortunate souls in the institution. Our fear of the incarcerated, not our potential connection through shared experience of the alienation of racism, neglect, or sadness, was the point of Scared Straight.

It was the most neoliberal thing. Perhaps the root of my teenage depression and clumsy attempts at misbehavior were a function of loneliness. My mother worked long, grinding hours, leaving me to catch brief glimpses of her in the mornings and later in the evening before she fell asleep, exhausted from the work and her long commute. They say that moving is a kind of traumatic event because of the uprooting that comes with it. Well, we moved every year from the end of sixth grade until I finally just moved away at the end of my sophomore year of high school. For other kids, the deprivation of their neighborhoods had also left them bored and wayward. There were so many other things that could be done to address our mutual sadness and troubles at school, but instead of doing those, they took us to the prison, in hopes of exposing us to a scene so awful that we would reform ourselves. No investments, no mentors, no programs. The fright of the prison was a much cheaper alternative. This was the eighties.

What I know now, many years later, is that the prison and what it represents is the real problem, not the people who have been confined to it. But that is part of the design. As Angela Y. Davis said in a talk more than twenty-five years ago,

> We have all learned how to forget about prisons, we push them into the background even if they're in our own neighborhoods. . . . We are afraid to face the realities of the prison industry even if we have friends and relatives in prison. In communities of color almost everybody knows someone who has been or is still in prison. But we have not learned how to talk about the centrality of prison in our lives. . . . We have not learned how to talk about prisons as institutions that collect and hide away the people whom society treats as its refuse . . . Prisons allow this society to discard people who have serious social problems rather than recognize that many of them are simply hurting themselves and are in need of help. They are simply thrown away.

That afternoon at Huntsville was meant to convince us to not become dead men walking, people with no past and no future, just souls adrift waiting out their time, waiting to die. It was meant to reinforce an idea that was growing in prevalence in the late nineteen eighties that young working-class people, especially if they were Black or Latino, who commit crimes deserve to be dispatched from society and deserve the cruelty that the institution of the prison, itself, has cultivated.

If we believe that there are people who deserve to be incarcerated in harsh conditions, then it is that much easier to elide the sociological and material explanations for crime that point to poverty, deprivation, boredom, anger, fear or depression, and other manifestations of social dislocation as reasons for crime. If we forgo those explanations, opting instead for the easier answer that dismisses crime as the result of bad people making bad choices, then there are few expectations for our society to create or facilitate the conditions for a better life for ordinary people.

Of course, there are many other crimes committed by the wealthy and elite that get ignored or that do not register in the public consciousness. There are the crimes of wage theft, charging rent for poorly maintained housing, polluting our air and water: a multitude of examples for which the criminal justice system would rarely intervene, let alone confine the perpetuators to the harsh conditions of the prison. In this way, our notions of what is criminal is deeply racialized and classed, meaning that the prison is seen as a place for the poor, working class, Black and Brown.

This powerful collection of poetry, *Like a Hammer*, brings the voices muffled by the thick walls and bars of the prison to life. It refuses the "common sense" that the imprisoned deserve the harshness that prison and state officials have encouraged and cultivated. If we listen, the incarcerated have something to say about life, love, politics, power, our world, and what to do about it. Their voices, this poetry, obliterates all that we have been told about the imprisoned, their families, their communities. The collection is not just from the incarcerated, but it also collects the writing of the formerly incarcerated and those who love them. The writing inspires but it also ignites and infuriates—because these are people who deserve to be freed from the prison, as do they all. No civilized society should rely upon the threat of violence, brutality, and banishment as a response to loneliness, sadness, hunger, and despair. I am now more convinced than ever before that the imprisoned are the true victims of our deranged society; this poetry is the evidence.

INTRODUCTION

How This Book Came to Be

Where I am from, the San Gabriel Valley, we don't talk about trauma. We talk about the gloves the neighbor put on her son during his wake to conceal the marks of torture by a rival gang. We talk about money and if there's enough to pay for Dad to attend his mother's funeral on a release in shackles. We listen to brothers, one of whom entered prison at fifteen and served more than a decade in the California Department of Corrections, consider from one end of a phone line an upcoming release date and whether or not Home Depot hires felons. *Like a Hammer: Poets on Mass Incarceration* comes from shared trauma. The unspoken kind that reverberates through lives across generations. This anthology explores how art and imagination can serve as vehicles for endurance, offering us the hope to envision a different future.

In 2018, I relocated to Tucson, Arizona, to work at the University of Arizona Poetry Center after spending over a decade in New York City. My poetry practice has been and will always be anchored in my experiences with the criminal justice system. I was only eight years old when my mother, brother, and I got arrested after my mother sold weed to narcs. I remember sitting in a holding cell wondering what was going to happen to us. That uncertainty connects me to this work—the untold stories of Brown and Black communities. The stories in this anthology must be heard. My move happened to coincide with the work of Agnes Gund, a philanthropist who launched the Art for Justice Fund in June 2017 in partnership with the Ford Foundation and Rockefeller Philanthropy Advisors to support criminal justice reform in the United States and who awarded the Poetry Center funding to commission a roster of poets to create work around the crisis of imagination, work meant to be a part of a lasting testament to these voices—this anthology. Gund knew that selling a single work of art—a Lichtenstein—could change lives.

We were writers on the inside and outside. Tyler Meier, executive director of the Poetry Center; Reginald Dwayne Betts, poet and lawyer; Kima Jones, writer and publicity partner; and I met regularly to select poets for this project. We spoke of those who were contributing important work and those who had experience with the criminal justice system—through teaching, direct influence, or otherwise. The commission given to these poets was to create new work in response to the crisis of mass incarceration, with the belief that these responses could support the reform of the criminal justice system and the idea that an anthology would be created. Later in the project, Kathie Klarreich—founder and executive director of Exchange for Change, a nonprofit that offers writing classes in South Florida correctional institutions and letter-writing exchanges with local public and private schools, colleges, and universities—brought to my attention the work of her students, poets on the inside, writing from experience. Poet Paola Valenzuela worked closely with me the last two years of the project, serving as an editorial assistant who supported and maintained the organizational framework for this work.

Collaborating with more than thirty poets over four years, I noticed their manuscripts were in conversation with one another, touching on topics like the loneliness of having a family member locked up, the despair of knowing you can't ever leave, and the contributing factor that the American justice system arose from a system of torture, not reform. Along with these subjects, the poets worried, "Do I have permission to write about the impact when I have never been inside?" "How can I authentically approach this subject?" The poets, who presented their work at the Poetry Center, traveled to Cape Detention Center, a juvenile court facility in Tucson, Arizona. Nikky Finney, a poet, led a deeply affecting poetry activity. She encouraged students to remember a nice memory that could serve as a charm for them to wear as protection. It demonstrated the power of art and how people call upon it in times of hardship.

How to Read This Book

Although it is unpopular to expect you to read this anthology from beginning to end (most anthologies are not meant to be read this way), I ask that you try. While this book contains chapters, sections, and demarcations of time, it is intended to be read as an endless journey, mirroring the perpetual nature of time that those inside experience—even if it means putting it down and picking it back up again. This will ensure that you acknowledge the grief and anguish we have inflicted on ourselves and one another through the carceral system. If you think about it, the idea of a book is peculiar. It's organized linearly, even though our lives do not unfold or lay down on a piece of paper. Because of this, although you should read this anthology from front to back, you should also read it as a constellation. Its shape, though fixed on the page, defies grounding and floats, lending itself more to a vast sky inhabited by the stars, or voices, in this book.

While ordering the work, I sought to showcase multiple viewpoints around a problem or topic, highlighting the ways that one poet sees something differs from how another poet sees it to produce a readable diversity, just as in life. The range of voices is vast, including an excerpt from a long poem titled *Visitations* from Patrick Rosal whose excerpt is performative, almost spiritual in nature, a disembodiment. The final section, which is devoted to Nikky Finney's poem "Still Life: Black Boy with Cow," is a crown of sorts, a culminating fifteen-page poem about fourteen-year-old George Stinney Jr., the youngest person to ever be electrocuted. Due to the poem's length, its meditative qualities on the loss of this young man's life, and his pain that can be felt years later, it comprises its own section and closes the book.

The Structure of the Book

In the first movement of the anthology, specifically in the first section "Time Rules This Empire," time takes center stage. This movement delves into the concept of time: the passage of time, the act of wasting it, and the contemplative act of understanding its significance. Additionally, it delves into the empire of our existence, viewing life as an accumulation of both our accomplishments and things we may have missed out on or regretted. These poems possess a philosophical and introspective nature and invite readers to contemplate a series of individual beliefs. They touch upon references to God and dive into the workings of the "empire" of their lives. Christopher Malec's poem "Which Is It?" highlights the architectural complexities of everyday existence and raises issues regarding the value of a person's existence when they witness their own life and death as two distinct entities interacting in a complex dance.

"Be Careful How You Speak about Rainbows," the second section, features poetry on flight and imagination: the yearning to experience the thrill of a flower, the body, a ray of light, or a bird's fleeting beauty. The range of these poems varies, and ends with Vanessa Angélica Villarreal's stanzas interrogating the historical context of this system, which comes from the same place that these poems do: the imagination, the European imagination, and its noxious assertion that through the veil of science, Brown and Black bodies are not spiritual bodies, but bodies to be defiled, if not reviled. Villarreal warns us not only about the future of the penitentiary system in the form of immigrant policing and detention camps, but also about its origins, which draw from the belief that anyone who was not European was not considered worthy of humane treatment. Section Three, "The Bill Is Past Due,"—titled after a line in Sin à Tes Souhaits's poem "10 Toes Down"—is about the everyday hustle to survive. In this section is John Murillo's long poem "The Ballad of Stagolee, or Variation on a Theme by Sterling A. Brown with a Slight Nod to Etheridge Knight:" a cinematic, dramatic rendering of a badass hero (framed as an epic) in Harlem, New York. "The Bill Is Past Due" also includes Candace Williams's poem "black, body" a rearrangement of WHREN v. UNITED STATES, 517 U.S. 806 (1996), and ends with a selection from a cycle of poems by Hanif Abdurraqib titled "All the TV Shows Are about Cops."

Section Four, aptly titled "American Inferno," focuses on life inside; both the environment and the architecture are meant to imprison. The idea of the penitentiary, its root word derived from the Latin *paenitentia* (repentance), has moved so far aways from its origin, as highlighted by the poems in this section. Each speaks to the vulnerability of a person in the face of brutality. This section is a place where you may read about what a mess we've caused, how we ridicule the idea of humanity by imprisoning people at such alarming rates, and how this escalation of entry has created not an escalation of thought about how we stop it, but an escalation of thought about how we monetize these persons through an inexpensive workforce.

"What Is Caged Is Also Kept from Us," Section Five, explores the human consequences of incarceration, not only on those who are put away but also on those who love and are forced to be separated from them, some for decades. The cost of this stress multiplies and tears families and individuals apart because of their helplessness to change the situation.

Closing the book is "Still Life: Black Boy with Cow" by Nikky Finney, an epic opus that merges personal essay, reportage, and lyric movements to remember the life of fourteen-year-old George Stinney Jr., the youngest person ever electrocuted. The poem is divided into two sections, Before and After; it leaves us awash with the damage that the criminal justice system has caused, the idea of what can be done to reverse such damage, and how can we absolve ourselves—not by looking to the past, but by looking for a different future.

These Words Can Make an Impact

As editor, I gathered some of the most powerful and engaging voices whose words would invite readers of all levels to gain something from these pages in order to take action, no matter how small. This anthology compiles some of the most intriguing material contributed, although it is only a small sampling of what has been written on the subject. While ordering the contributions, it was important not to prioritize one poem over another but rather to consider the poems' content, mood or tone, and perspective. *Like a Hammer* is presented here with the intention that this crisis of imagination, incarceration, will continue until we can imagine ourselves without prisons.

While the legal system may appear established and unchangeable, art has the power to question dominant narratives, reveal injustices, and organize communities in support of reform. Art can raise awareness, shift public opinion, and mobilize collective action. The creative work assembled here evoke emotions, conveys crucial messages, amplifies minority voices, and provides alternate viewpoints. It is a forum for narrative, self-expression, and critical thought. I hope this book will elicit empathy, stimulate conversation, and compel social change initiatives.

Diana Marie Delgado
July 4, 2023

I.

Time Rules This Empire: Where Clocks Stand Still

Randall Horton

: .Or. This *Malus* Thing Never to Be Confused with Justice

nothing symbolic. okay. dark is dark—
  cage is cage. hunted & hunter are both
in the literal. make believe & *what ifs*
  do not exist: a lie. nothing cryptic here.
okay. rape is rape. prey must pray. no
  minute in the future safe from quiet
insertions of a shank in masking tape.
  okay. nothing here infinite: only time
is constant to the merciful & merciless—
  there are no allegories to hide behind.
he slit his wrists means he slit his fuckin wrists
okay? there is a cell with one window
  just before day. dawn's early demise
magnifies a dull metal toilet. the cool
  water cooling two can sodas. each
wall a slab of soft gray cinderblock, no
posters featuring eroticized women
with an exclusive in BLACK TAIL. okay.
  the wall that slits the light does not
reveal nothing new, ever. the exposé
  the changing same: always a holding.
one window offers a gateway. my face
  pressed against the window & time
rules this empire. okay. the mind held
  hostage by time. mind & body
conjoined twins. the other wall holds
  a frame. the frame holds a metal door
to contain utter disbelief. of the visible:
  walls are gray not like summer
but darker—*yes. there is darkness.* okay?

Hanif Abdurraqib

All the TV Shows Are about Cops

when everything else fails the imagination,
cruelty is one way to pass the time.

place a blacklight over a hood so violent
the officers stopped coming years before

I was born & you will see the fingerprints
of everyone who'd hoped we'd bury ourselves

in time for condos to go on sale.
I knew the boys who put bullets through the window

of the pizza shop on Livingston with their father's
gun. it was the summer their parents got laid

off like everyone else, phones ringing in the dead
& humid air of morning & then a box

on the doorstep, overflowing with old family
photos. me & mine know all the ways to make a loaf of bread

& a jar full of peanut butter last. ketchup
and a slice of cheese if you can score one.

smirk when the mc tells us to *get our bread up.*
in the courtroom the boys said they pulled

the trigger because they were afraid — of what,
who knows. the shots missed the owner,

who put up his hands holding three 20s
& whispering *this is all I have.*

maybe that was the fear all along—
setting out to make a fortune & marching back

home with less than a paycheck's worth
of dough while the heat from a fired gun

burned through tattered jeans.
this, too, is a type of ruin. break the bread

or be broken by it. point the weapon before
knowing how to keep it on safety.

nothing safe: not the 9 to 5 that breaks
the backs of your people, not the grocery store

hanging on by a thread, not even the summer itself
or the water hoses hung high & dripping into dry-mouthed

hoopers and hop-scotchers. what small slice of the world
do you love enough to tear apart with your bare hands.

what scarce feeling have you folded
over to make last. what sticky heat

have all your worst losses been buried under.
the families might starve whether they gotta visit you behind bars or not.

Sin à Tes Souhaits

TRAP noun. \'trap\

noun. \'trap\
   1. a device or enclosure designed to catch and retain or to kill animals, typically by allowing entry but not exit or by catching hold of a part of the body; see also "CAGE"; see also "SHACKLE"
   As in: If an animal is caught in a trap, it will probably die there.

   2. an unpleasant situation from which it is hard to escape; a trick by which someone is misled into acting contrary to their interests or intentions; see also "RESPECTABILITY"; see also "MASCULINITY"; see also "SCARCITY"; see also "WHITE SUPREMACY"
   As in: Even an exceptionally smart or strong animal can fall into a trap. As in: Genius is a trap.

   3. residential areas with predominantly Black populations that have been historically impoverished and blocked from fair access to healthcare, housing, educational resources, and jobs, and disproportionately patrolled by law enforcement; see also "GHETTO"; see also "PROJECTS"; see also "HOOD"
   As in: The trap is home to too much genius that will probably die there.

verb. \'trap\
   1. catch (an animal) in a trap; see also "AMBUSH"; see also "ARREST"
   As in: To trap you need a victim.

   2. prevent (someone) from escaping from a place; have

(something, typically a part of the body) held tightly by
something so that it cannot move or be freed; see
also "REDLINE"; see also "JAIL"
As in: When you trap something, you are the God
of its movements.

3. engage in extralegal activities necessitated by lack
of access to sustainable wages, fair housing,
affordable education, and healthcare; see also
"PUSH"; see also "MOVE"; see also
As in: We trap in the trap cause we trapped.

Rhionna Anderson

Marriage

Your raw emotions are rare,
they keep me focused
Never think in a crowded room,
you'd go unnoticed
Then I wake up
You're no longer there
You're gone and I'm scared
Close my eyes in search of you
This can't be true
All I see is four walls,
I'm locked in a cell
Pick up the phone
You're no longer there
This becomes my reality
The sadness is suffocating
And the separation kills all hope
of ever reuniting

Christopher Malec

Which Is It?

      this is life
hiding behind the alphabet of conjecture
expanding into chaos with an index
cometting straight for inexistence
kicked by a god doing God's job
      this is death
crawling careless through conscious
eating into the sides of calendar boxes
unforgiven under the macroscopic lens
a parasite feeding off the nature of rebellion
      this is life
sleeping under the covers of purgatory
tucked in tight with fresh cement
never waking any closer to an end
but reprieve escaping the lie of dreams
      this is death
wearing a four-letter oxymoronic prank
juking poster-sized picket-sign displays
absconding headlines in politic disguise
every executioner has a hood to lower
      this is life
by name
      this is death
in truth
      this is death
ensued
      this life
           without a soul

Vanessa Angélica Villarreal

Architect 1

"In the Middle Ages the New World, like southern Africa, was convincingly *physically uninhabitable* to Europeans. Upon encounters, and alongside Descartes's newly mathematizable world and Copernican theory, the question of humanness became wrapped up in the differences between Man's embodiment of the image of God and the New World inhabitants. The physical sciences and new struggles over religious frameworks (new heavens, new earths, a moving planet) produced a reasonable Man, located between 'the lower natures of brutes' and divine natures. Here, human Others—inside and outside Europe—were identifiable 'enemies of Christ,' irrational and abnormal; the creed-specific, seemingly universal, conception of the human was a natural and rational 'Godded' Man." —Katherine McKittrick, *Demonic Grounds*

1641. What will become the prison begins in Europe, in the mind of Descartes:

cogito ergo sum. In regarding the New World and its peoples, the European man is thrown into crisis. All he thought he knew

of humanness is destabilized at the sight of the Black and indigenous body, its physicality—*surely they aren't also human, surely I am not like them*—and so he turns inward to make sense of the world. He rebuilds reality from the anchor of the thought, and in thinking himself, radically separates mind from body into dual natures: angel and animal, pure soul and bestial body. This is the birth of the white imaginary, the construction of white identity central to Western consciousness and its dualism of Reason over Nature.

Reason alone makes us men and distinguishes us from the beasts: the thinking European Man as fundamentally different from "unthinking" nature. No longer bound to a collective consciousness, Reason places man above nature—just as mind controls body, so does Man control the physical world and the nature-bound body of unmapped terrain; a slight metaphysical shift that forms the worldwide structure of oppression and in doing, produces the consciousness that will rupture the world.

Forgive me these abstractions—I am speaking from the end of this timeline; I am looking for the origin of the worldwound, the seismic shift in consciousness that estranged us from each other and continues to produce the present, the prison, the border; I am speaking from the burning rainforest, the rising ocean, the atrocities of our dying future.

To locate the site of rupture, I must investigate the scene of the crime: Europe,

PART I: TIME RULES THIS EMPIRE | 17

the origin of a consciousness that cannot imagine a world without prison, police, supremacy.

The radical separation of mind from body fundamentally remakes reality—mind over matter is serious business, a dualism that will entrench colonial logic

into the sciences just as they are developing and documenting the life and matter of the universe, imagined through masculine Reason over the animalistic, feminized, nature-

bound body. Reason over nature produces the supremacy of the European Man in contrast to the irrational colonial subject, the axis of difference upon which the New World is built, mapped,

peopled, labored, gendered: fertile coasts, virgin territories, vulnerable to ships sailing the Cartesian plane across a world splitting in two.

Reason dismantled our collective conscience and shared knowledge systems; when Man encounters the unknown, all difference is made *irrational* to make Man coherent,

obliterating the colossal mystery of our planet, reduced to a dim blue seed. His divine intelligence defined against the irrational animal will go on to invent race, himself the angel above

the *brute*, the *monster*, the *savage*, the *prisoner*, the *slave*, diminishing complex ecospiritual agriculture, advanced astronomical navigation

to the limits of his perception; intricate social systems of kinship lost
to skeptical, simplistic binaries; a reality structured by antagonism, empirical

evidence, the burden of proof. Science and law will produce the animal body as *suspect,
criminal, fugitive* alongside the prison. Reason is the domain of empire,

its function to set Man's gaze on the horizon of expansion,
that, in preserving itself, criminalizes the world.

Another seismic shift: in reorienting the world in Man, difference becomes permanent—
Blackness, the savage, the heathen, the feminine, the base, the queer, the contagion;

Reason produces the *condition* of difference as inherent, the Other is always *not* him;
for the European man to exist, he must always be defined against difference,

every encounter an estrangement instead of recognition, reminding each of the war,
the Othered never satisfying the gaze that unmakes the world.

From the same mind: *cogito ergo sum* as point of origin (0, 0)
on a cross x/y axes that go on, infinitely—

This is not a neutral geometry. On the Cartesian plane, empire thinks itself
into existence as the center of infinite expansion, dual hemispheres of unequal power,

mapping reality as property, as capital, as resource, as inheritance
for the European man, a crown infinitely possible in any direction.

Inextricable: human from European, knowledge from colony, science from race.
Benefactor of empire, what hubris to shift consciousness from world to self,

To shift truth from belonging to the world to the European man alone,
himself the judge and all else subject to judgement—

Power is the insistence of what one believes to become everyone's truth.
And so this reality was mapped onto the Cartesian plane, along axes of difference:

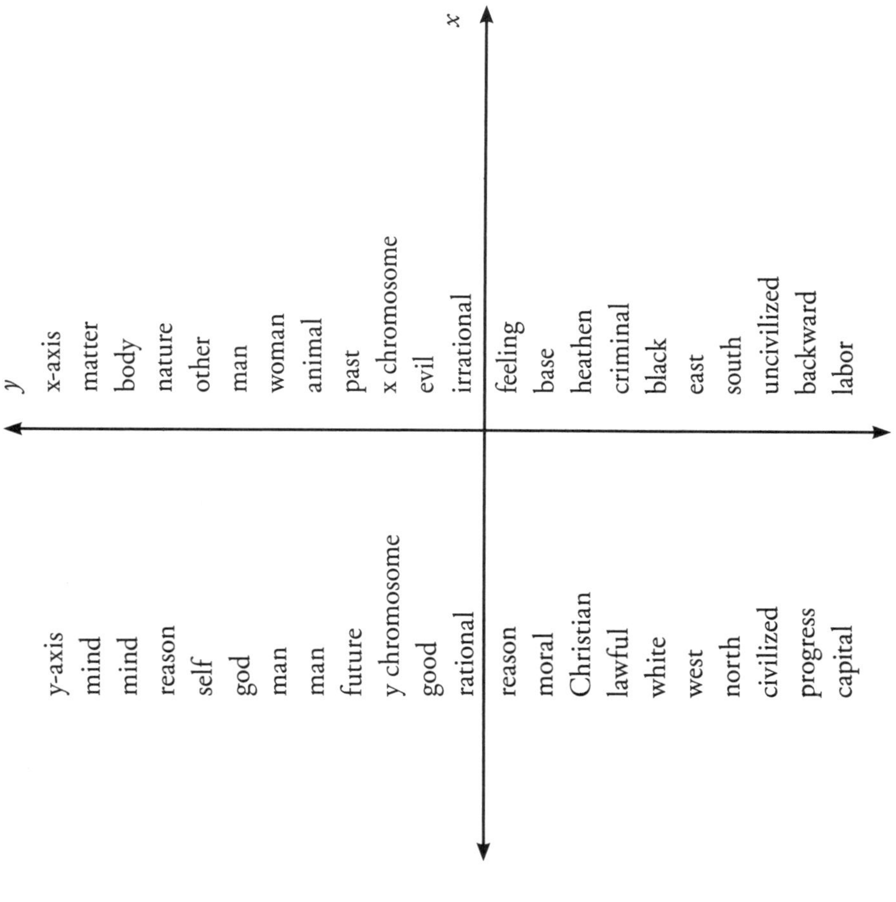
y
x
y-axis x-axis
mind matter
mind body
reason nature
self other
god man
man woman
man animal
future past
y chromosome x chromosome
good evil
rational irrational
reason feeling
moral base
Christian heathen
lawful criminal
white black
west east
north south
civilized uncivilized
progress backward
capital labor

Man doesn't evolve to Reason; Reason imagines difference to create Man as superior, tearing reality in two to build an empire of fear, always requiring subjugation to produce the self, borders to produce space, gender to produce labor; a consciousness built on fear that makes a world in which we are ever more not like each other, and in so doing, makes all the world a cell.

Reginald Dwayne Betts

Blood History

Some things get   remembered different; precise,
as the English tongue   can be, with words
like *petrichor* & *perseverate*   ain't no
sequence of letters   to describe this leaving.
Years ago, inside   a cell we shared
Juvie wondered   if I'd longed for a
father. Had he said   wanted, I'd've
dismissed my brother   the way young'uns
dismiss it all: a shrug, sarcasm, a sharp
jab to the stomach,   laughter. But he said
longing. & in a different   place, I might
have wept & said   my father lived
with us & then he didn't   & it messed me up
so bad, I ain't think   about his leaving
until I held   my first born in my arms
& only now   speak on it. Once, a man
who drink whiskey   & Wild Irish Rose
like water, tells a circle   of black boys
that ain't no word   for father where he
from, not like we know: *There, the word father*
is the same as the word   *for listen*. The blunts
we passed around   let us abandon
our tongues. Not like   though. But imagine
the liquor ain't lie,   & if you have no
father you can't hear   straight. Years later, mine
says to me: *son,*   *why your firstborn ain't got*
our name, as if he   ain't know, some things turn
your life into a prayer   the gods will certainly answer.

Sandra Jackson

Lost

   I'm shattered by lost, pain, and betrayal.
I hate that I wasn't aware of what
was going on when I wasn't home. "How
could I be so blind?" I wake everyday,
these past 11 years, thinking this thought.
   No one can say anything about me
as a mother that I haven't said to
myself. No one knows what I was going
through at that time and place. It
doesn't change the fact that I left
my children with the guy that should
have been man enough to stand by my
side, to hold me up.
   Instead, he was the one to shatter
me. When people ask if "I'm ok" I say
"Yes" even when it's not true. How can
I be "ok" when I've lost my son and
am not allowed to see my girls, to
know that they have grown up with
out me, not able to make sure that
they know they were not what was
wrong in my life.
   They were the best things I
ever did.
   To write to see how they are
and never get an answer about what
I asked. I go to bed thinking about
the fact that I can no longer tell
my children goodnight, or see their sweet
faces. It's my fault this is: I
should have been home those nights.

Natalie Diaz

Under Correction I

When I visit the correctional facility
to see my sister, I do not get to see her.
I watch a television of her.

My sister is scripted as a new character.
Together we're the program's live and captive audience—
only my sister is captured.

My real, untelevised sister is somewhere on the other side
of the screen. I am somewhere on this side
of the screen. We are figures across a distance,

over a net of cyclone fence and static—we are playing
tennis on a state-sponsored cable channel, with no ball
or racket, no wealthy white people in the stands,

and no one will call out to us: *Love-Love.*

My sister is broadcast to me
from a satellite transmitter in the sky,
but she isn't as far from me as they want her to seem.

My sister is approximately 400 feet away, locked up
in this box within a box—a settler colonial magic show.
Not sawed in half, but close: a Hans Moretti sword box.

Where is the illusion—is it us? Or is it freedom?
Now you see your sister, and now you don't.
Whose sister can climb out of this box uninjured?

My sister does because we know this complex.
We were born with it and our Certificates of Indian Blood.
My sister and I have an industrial complex—

and today, maybe every day, we're in the same complex
and complicated. From behind the black bubble camera
dripping like an ink blot from the ceiling corner,

a guard or three keep violent vigil, watch me watch
a symbol of my sister. From that distance,
my sister and I are a performance of people,

but not real people. One of us is acting the part
of the good guy. One of us is acting the part
of the bad guy. We are performing

both the stage and the audience, the ushers,
the trapdoor, the gaffs, the curtains falling.
We are performing the architecture

of a concrete block and a Nation. My sister needs
to be a stone, and I am learning to be a mountain.
Though we are both quarried.

Inside this inside we are each less-than
and outside. Inside we are un-bodies, fastasmas
of an unlivable life that isn't the life we live.

They took my sister's glasses from her,
because our country has a vision, and it corrects us
until we see it. Read the line: N, D, N, and U, S, A.

My sister and I have been corrected to a safe distance,
to watch a television from. We are in the books,
edited and revised. *My sister and I* is a sentence,
                                        corrected.

Christina Pernini

Behind the Wall

Heaven be my hell,
hell be my place.
The angels I've seen;
gone without a trace.
Blinded by beauty,
avenged by their rage.
A cunning delusion,
trapped in this cage.
Do not cry for me,
I am but a mime.
Forever free in this box,
my own version of time.

II.

Be Careful How You Speak about Rainbows: Beauty & Grace

Eduardo Martinez

A.G.A.M.

let's shut the government down
                      isn't that a revolutionary purpose?
this is America, not Venezuela
                      oils important not the Chico's
Euros are still worth more than dead presidents
pompous pouting, hair spray fake tan poker faces
                      Trumps power everything in gambling
U.S. treasury performing plastic surgery cutting credit
                                cosmetic congress
movements are scripted movies
                take what you want
campaign Champaign shower locker room talk
                boys will be boys
clutching kittens female feline scared purrs
        every swine has a pearl necklace on
it's a trend   like racial sober slurs
    let's all scream
    "METOO"
before they toe tag the #tags
be careful how you speak about rainbows
they know how to weather a storm
                a pot of gold is an American idol
melted into religious charms
12 pack trophies in a gangster's smile
                are those real, or pull-outs?
don't tell us settle down
                the lost tribes tried and died
college kids mocking Indians on CNN
political pilgrims pardoning turkeys on thanksgiving
        why not the children in prison?
it's against tradition
        you mean, there's no dirty dishes in your kitchen
Mexican housekeepers cleaning mansions of evil spirits

     who said the Clintons weren't reptilians?
  some slippery serpent slithered past Bernie
we've all been bitten by pediatricians
    first part of our programming
     before our eyes dived inside televisions
let's step out the static
and come to the light
     where's the lil' old lady in poltergeist
  clairvoyant guidance, not *Siri*
a jittery upcoming generation, writing diaries
in concrete attics with Anne Frank's haunted ink pen
under a suburb of trailer homes by an underground railroad
    where ghetto dwellers are railroaded
forearm tracks covered by tats
    no boarding pass on the runaway train
just slaves chucking diamonds, blowing steam
   we'll all end up wearing filter faces
like the Chinese just to breathe
  first class clouds
viewing coyotes challenging road runners to a foot race
across a fiscal cliff
    what's a life inside a penal system
    a provocation of soulful suicide
paint your face black
   be careful now, it might stay like that
   like crossing eyes when crossing crossroads
   when your vision's already crooked as a political
   prisoner with a platinum spoon perspective
Welfare silverware
there's malice in a poor man's wooden chalice
   but he isn't the bar tender
  refills aren't free
when being half empty is trending
   going viral can be vital or vice-versa
they, you know, *they*, that are not you
    do a real head count every six years
6.1 million Felons digesting disrespect
   of an upper classes content

                  and those are outdated statistics
everything in America multiplies towards worse
Gremlin children
    being force fed lies after midnight
let's pledge with our left hands
petitioning to free God
who's wearing prison stripes behind bars of the flag
                  bullet hole stars
hey, you think our spangled banner
    is still posted swaying on the moon?
let's find out, with Google goggle eyes
    then hitchhike to Mars
where we'll all swan dive singing swan songs
                and belly flop
                and land on the other side of the border wall
we won't know who's alien then
'cause ain't no *Annunakis* on those caravans
    a Richard Nixon kind of peace sign
who needs pesticide?
when genocide has low-income communities screaming
    RAID!
    when the cops pull up
soon enough, blood drive trucks will be pulling drive-bys
    there's kid snatchers now
    not dog catchers
be careful how you speak about animals
pink poodles can be sensitive to certain verbatim
    Speciesism
but, say what you want about the human vermin
    that are locked up
        they lost their hearts to a Masonic judge
            now they keep their feelings
                in a mason jar
devouring them in rations
    when irrational people put wrong labels on them
        who gets full on feelings anyways . . .
        or memories,
                besides the Incarcerated

who's narrating this deflating nation from within . . .
ahem ahem ahem
jail cell speaker of the house
a newborn
with his *M.A.G.A* cap flipped backwards
AMERICAS.GOVERNMENT.AGAINST.MINORITIES
empathy has no bond
or a paid lawyer
5.7 billion for a border
isn't that hangman slang for framed
i'm ready to jump out this picture
too many colors disagreeing   besides
who's that wall really for?
a Panopticon design
to keep a suspenseful suspicious lens on us
truth, will shoot straight up your nose
synthetic drug chemical warfare
catch a drain
numb your soul and swallow it
spit overdose mathematics
72,200
pharmaceutical trafficking
causing traffic jams in young mentals
we've all got potential   to be cut off
and miss the streets
and experience road rage inside cages
HEY LADY!
gold digger with the blindfold on,
you got a beast growing in your belly,
marked with an institutional ID,
another UPC barcode
keep eating us like hors d'oeuvres
you'll get sick one day
and throw us all back up
then what
return to your vomit
like a proverb or a poem
no one reads into anymore or let alone believes in

        like a government shutdown
                sitting on death row

Catherine LaFleur

Bloom

Arrival came in the sun
the garden spills over races
all the way to the back gate.

My legs among daffodils glowing
pale prison white with the Iris
blocking my escape.

Other inmates
surround-sound me, a squabble of
hens complain about heat, sun, thirst, hunger.

Yet I am alone, jaw hung my gaze
palm and hibiscus dazed
flower heads nodding companionable.

Doubt seeps from my fingers
drains out of toes. I bend down and
pluck a cheerful yellow bloom.

I tuck it behind my ear
ready for intake into this
prison of flowers.

Marcelo Hernandez Castillo

Eclogue: A Field Guide and Cure

1.

Walking seven miles around Folsom prison
my job, for it is a job, is to document plants
and log their curative properties.
Sweet fennel, black locust, yerba santa, dove weed,
chaparral broom, eastern redbud, sweet gum.

A Schemata:

$$\text{if}$$
$$\{Maps - borders = debt\}$$
$$\text{then}$$

What could they have healed for whom
there is no healing?

2.

I am required to tell you
I have a cousin serving life
without parole in Folsom prison.

In your imagination of his crime,
for you have already imagined it,
there must be a gold bell.
It behooves you
to imagine it ring and the rain that follows.

3.

It rained and we did nothing about it—
the court said there is no further explanation needed.

4.

His time and his nails
like blue division.
As in departing from a common source.
A house inside another house—
we arrive: If
                {*tragedy* + *time* = *comedy*}
                        Then
                six hummingbirds are nailed to a wall.

The prison museum named The Big House
in bold italics.

5.

My brother remodeled the prison kitchen—
pots as big as a bath bolted to the floor,
biggest he'd ever seen.
Ungodly heavy.

6.

I went to school where the football stadium
was also called The Big House and where
people screamed and screamed.
        If
{*Comedy* - *time* = *tragedy*}
        then

7.

There is shame here but not
how you imagine it.

Black sunflower seeds evenly
Placed on a table,

The sound of them opening and closing
    if and only if

$$\{Shame - Comedy = Time\}$$

8.

Unlike those I saw on the trail,
how ungodly large and heavy
the redbud and the dogwood were in biblical times.

The dogwood used to crucify the Son of God,
the redbud used by His traitor, Judas, to hang himself in shame.
Henceforth, both trees, in their unique guilt
never again grew large enough to hold a body,
their branches henceforth too thin
to ever hang from, and their petals, no longer white,
but red in spring.

Henceforth named the Judas tree.

9.

Mile after mile. Febrifuge, black locust for fever.
Eaten for the tumors that grow
in whatever empty space is left in your body.
Emetic. Analgesic to move the pain
in your mouth in circles
until it feels like stirring a large pot
of warm broth in winter.

Mile three ushered, and the gold bell ringing mad only if
                              $\{Wealth + Comedy \geq Madness\}$

You are lovely in the eyes of the state.

10.

Gum bush, California Yerba Santa—
The lips of the hanged Judas
unable again to defile with a kiss the most holy—

A tincture and tea from the bark
to stimulate the respiratory system,
treats chronic asthma or

        {Breath - Time > Tragedy}

11.

Henceforth my job is to imagine a crime
absolved by the oils of sweet gum—
emmenagogue, carminative—anointed,
the hummingbird now no longer turning its head—
in deference of madness.

12.

The court recommends an explanation.

So be it, the manicured trail named after Johnny Cash's
famous visit has polite cyclists
on expensive bikes and public art.

A cold infusion for the common flu and congestion.

Mile after ungodly mile. White flowers. Red flowers.
Some kind of peppermint.

Consumptive weed ingested to terminate pregnancy.
Its same feathery seeds at one time used to stuff baby toys.

13.

Henceforth each mile through the town center's prison aesthetic—
bridges designed with decorative guard towers, rusted grates,
and hedge-walls lined with the same
quarried stones used to build the prison—
a rustic panopticon charm.

Galactogogue, carminative.

14.

$$\frac{Tragedy + Repetition > \underline{Permanence}}{Tragedy}$$

15.

Dear cousin, this is the closest I can and have ever come.
Biggest pots I'd ever seen. Ungodly heavy.
Of course wildly capable,
Febrifuge, analgesic and the scent of almonds.

16.

Of course, wildly funded public art
and the nearby antique shops
that sell the collateral damage
of outdated restraints
long after they've outlived
their usefulness and practice.

As in use: as in use this for that.
The restorative power of your life set to a score.
Emenagogue, galactogogue, laxative.
Both a purge and hunger to know your best self
in your best starched shirt in your best ironed pants.
Lemon Scented Gum Tree to keep the mosquitos away.

Mile after ungodly mile,
More shiny bicycle thank-you's.
Emollient as an atoned self portrait of the landscape.

Henceforth
[Cheers from the inmates]
[Cheers from the guards holding Mary Magdalene]
[Cheers and screaming and more cheers and more screaming]

Unknown Variable ± Beauty
[Standard Deviation ± 2]

17.

Even though Folsom Lake has dried up, the beachside homes
have firmly maintained their value [more cheers].

More lemon scented gum. The blood and blood you gave
which made way for a bewildering path
I could never follow.

18.

The last adjacent mile to you.
The last bird thrumming like a nervous finger, [more cheers]
deranged by the absence of cardinal points—
the useless instruments in the stamens
to lose direction on good and heavy legal paper.

Febrifuge, antispasmodic—
dear cousin, dear son, idle brother,
your blue opera swimming down river,
your greatest good of the bronze redemption.

I document the oldest tree in existence.
I run into a bell flower,
I run into a field and clamor of bells.

Kennedy A. Gisege

Scattered Like Yellow Feathers

I stand among flowers
scattered like the yellow
feathers of a yellow bird
then start to go crazy
with a terrible flowering
of madness thinking
about a night disturbed by
pleasure of a girl who
absconded with a dowry
priced with fruiting breasts
I wonder about her thighs
rolled up with sweetness
now lost forever like
a yellow bird in flight.

Roque Raquel Salas Rivera

En las primeras décadas del nuevo siglo[1]

Endless letting go, endless looking
                              else-
where, endless turning out to be
otherwise...
      —Nathaniel Mackey

Cenex se puso en marcha,
pero, en ese siglo betún,
había cometido un delito
digno de castigo, un robo
de arroz y café o una deuda
de grano, ron y tierra.
La justicia, siempre excelsa,
lx encontró a pie en el camino Real
sediente de fuente.
Y, aunque en el Artículo 1.
quedaba prohibida la extracción
de esclavos sin permiso Real,
el Artículo 2.1 exceptuaba
los sentenciados por los tribunales.

Le transportaron ante aquel cajón
de la zafra, con su estalactita pendiente,
donde las guardias revisaban los reclusos.
Una detallaba los procedimientos
y la otra los desvestía.

---

1   Incluye fragmentos de "Convención entre España y Holanda para restituirse mutuamente los desertores y fugitivos de sus colonias Americanas" (23 de Junio de 1791); "Carta de Don Ignacio de Ramón Carbonell a su hermana sobre un viaje a Puerto Rico," (5 enero 1845); y "Circular del Gobernador Fernando de Norzagaray Prohibiendo la Extracción de Esclavos de la Isla de Puerto Rico" (7 marzo 1854).

La española con voz tallada explicaba
mientras la gringa supervisaba la fila.
Una repetía con tono compareciente,
y la otra los miraba con odio fijo
y manoseo firme.
La estructura en sí, se debatía.
El estilo Neomudéjar, con su afán secular,
contenía un corazón vacío de reforma,
una gran plaza de ciudad española,
sembrada de flores fugitivas.

Roque Raquel Salas Rivera

In the First Decades of the New Century[2]

> *Endless letting go, endless looking*
> *else-*
> *where, endless turning out to be*
> *otherwise. . .*
>
> —Nathaniel Mackey

Cenex began their march,
but in this bitumen century
they had committed a felony
worth punishment, a theft
of rice or coffee or a debt of
grain, rum or land.
Justice, always lofty,
found Cenex on the Royal
road, thirsty for a source.
And, although Article 1.
states the extraction of slaves is
prohibited without Royal decree,
Article 2.1 makes an exception
for those sentenced by tribunals.

They were transported before that crate
of harvest, with its dangling stalactite,
where the guards checked inmates.
One detailed the procedures and

---

2 Includes fragments from "Convention between Spain and Holland for the mutual restoration of deserters and fugitives from their American colonies" (June 23, 1791); "Letter from Don Ignacio de Ramón Carbonell to his sister regarding a trip to Puerto Rico" (January 5, 1845); and "Circular from Governor Fernando de Norzagaray prohibiting the extraction of slaves from the island of Puerto Rico" (March 7, 1854).

the other handled undressing.
The Spaniard with a carved voice explained,
while the gringa supervised the line.
One repeated a tone appearing before
the other with a fixed hate
and a firm hand.

The structure itself, debated.
The Neo-Mudéjar style, its secular toil,
contained a heart free of reform,
a great plaza for a Spanish city,
planted with fugitive flowers.

Tongo Eisen-Martin

Knees Next to Their Wallets

Fast cash smuggled through my infant torso
                              I arrived smiling
          Coral check-cashing spots seal my eyes

        Hearing voices,
                but none of them sing to me

                I am lucky to be a metaphor for no one

            A Greek philosopher takes the path of least resistance
                        The bronze corporation age dawns

                In board rooms, they ask if county line skin
                    can be churned directly into cornflakes

                      A senate's special chain gang mines
        our neighborhood for evidence of continent unity

                    Makes a mess of the word "kin"

          System makes a psychic adjustment

                          Makes a war report
             out of a family's secret chord progression

                    Makes white people geniuses

Lynch mob freaks rehearse their show tunes
in the courthouse walls that they take for mirrors
Rehearse for a president's pat on the head
A pat on the head
that they take for audience laughter

A lot of "sirs" in the soup
A lot of speed

Treaty ink stained teeth
write themselves a grin

Imperialist speech writers' grins
boil over in my ink-riddled mind

A non-future dripping with real people
I mean, real people…Not poem people

        A street with no servants somehow
        A soul singer/somehow in the west
        Consolation eternity
        or
        The poor man's fish order
        This half of a half of a spirit
        Or husk of a messiah
            Religious memorabilia made from the wood of
a farm fence
            For sibling domestic colonies and the
        not-for-profit Tuesday meltdowns
            We do straightforward time

Plot twists provided by white beggars
In a black city
The fathers who Reagan flicked
Kicking garbage thinking about rates of production
Notebooks dangling out of car windows

            We Go the way of
            Now-extinct hand gestures

Mediterranean sandals and underground moods in tandem
        I mean, whoever I am today is still your friend

Crooked cops and crooked news junkies
Diallo is your mind on military science
      Is from your monotheistic toy collection

if you turn down the television low enough, you can hear San Francisco
begging for more war profiteering

if it wasn't for San Francisco
there wouldn't have been a transatlantic slave trade

We will not live forever, but someone out there wants us to

      We are mice pouring through an hour glass
           In Olympus, Babylon
           Or Babylon, Olympus

              subway car smoke session
        making its way into an interrogation room
           (Maybe it is all just one room.
            It's definitely all just one smoker)

            Poor people writing letters
          near books about Malcolm X
              Ice pick in the art
            new floor boards for
              Watts prophesy
        Pen twitching over scrap paper
           Pen tweaking while
Smoothly a bus driver delivers incarcerated children

              The Lord's door opens

Erica "Ewok" Walker

D.O.C. "department of castration"

Sensory deprivation
Censored Imagination
Intimacy unauthorized
sightless through shaded eyes
Spiceless sustenance
Odorless fields of shes
Wandering inside an onyx abyss
Hearts faintly beating
Whispered pleas escape their lips
Brain activity in a muted state
Dysfunctional, Hopeless, Alone
A vast unknown
Our names are numbers
Possessions not our own
Concrete Walls
No place to call home
Society's graveyard, Pariahs
Blue shrouds cover our bones
Inadequate, not human
Time eludes the staggering souls
Defined by a single episode
Apocalyptic visions, a welcome mode
Injustice, justified by men in black robes
Spirits burned by hot coals
Dousing a future we'll never know
Drowning in a pool of sorrow
Unable to breathe
Won't see tomorrow

III.

The Bill Is Past Due: The Hustle

Sin à Tes Souhaits

10 Toes Down

i leave home in the three-thirty dark
while the desert is still cold & breathe
the clean dirt smell risen by the rain. i try
to find a formula for the grind: slide on
my Poormans & skate six miles to work; stash
the extra in the duffle & keep both
eyes on the bag. if i make five at lunch
that's fifty. need twelve a day for the rent
on the first. can only afford four hours sleep.
i have gotten better at math than hoping
the numbers will add up in my favor or
even be equal. i no longer care how
much my body must be taxed before i can
be free. the bill is past due.

Leeann Parker

If I Were a Boy

Just for today.
Would you still yell demean and
disrespect me or would you be more
careful with the words that you say.
Would you still scream "Hey Inmate
get in line tuck in your shirt or shut
your mouth," or would you take a
second and pause, Because we are
both equal and powerful in our own right.
If I were a boy even Just for today
Would there still be sexual abuse Just
because you're In Charge of me and I
have to listen to what you say.
Would you still Threaten to lock me up
And slam me on the ground or
Because, of my height and width
Would that be enough to make
you take a second to think and look around.
I will tell you what I would do
If I were a Boy even Just for today,
I would take back all the power
you have taken from us Just because
We are women and you feel like you
have the right to take it away.
I would lift my head turn my Back
and walk away and continue on with
All the pride I have managed to save
and courage to do what we have all
wanted to do every single day.
Just walk away even Just for today.

John Murillo

The Ballad of Stagolee, or Variation on a Theme by Sterling A. Brown with a Slight Nod to Etheridge Knight

I.

Hear ye, Hear ye!
    Pull up a chair and sit still.
I got bubble gum and time
    and a story to tell.

Well I'm fresh out of gum
    and have someplace I gotta be.
But listen close, I'll be quick
    about my main man, Stagolee.

Now once upon a midnight
    Stagolee left the house
of Harlem's finest, grinning
    cat with the proverbial mouse.

You won't believe it but pimping Stag
    for once thought he might
put a ring on the last woman
    he bedded that night.

He thought about her smile,
    thought about her lips,
thought about her wide
    west African hips.

Stag stopped to light a square,
    thinking about her hair,
and heard, "Nigger, drop that cig
    and get your hands in the air!"

The king was interrupted
    ruminating 'bout his queen
by six cops in one car,
    pointing guns and looking mean.

They had blue guns, black guns,
    long guns, short guns.
All sorts of guns.
    Don't-show-up-in-the-report guns.

Stagolee stood steady
    in the streetlamp glow,
Blowing smoke O's
    and leaned against the pole.

He thought to himself,
    "These motherfuckers must
Got me confused for an
    unarmed black man. Trust,

I'm Stago-fucking-lee,
    with the wild fo'-fo'.
'Bout to send six rockets
    through these pigs' car do'."

Just then a cop shouted,
    "Nigger, can't you hear?!"
Stag said, "Naw, suh, I caint.
    Could you come a little nearer?"

A crowd started forming,
    coming closer to see.
One woman whispered,
    "Do they know they fucking with Stagolee?"

The wrinkled one, used to
    keeping Blacks under boot,
used to smacking around

and shaking down for loot,

stepped his old ass
    out the car, he did,
his old bones creaking.
    Then he started speaking:

"Boy, you must don't recognize
    the badges and the car.
You must not see the gats.
    You know who we are?

You know where you at?
    When we say stick your hands up,
you stick 'em." Another cop said,
    "Let's beat him and kick him."

The other four cops
    hopped out the funky ride,
slid their pistols into holsters,
    pulling whackers from their side.

One shouted, "Show ID!"
    One hollered, "Hands in the air!"
One bellowed, "Butt on the ground!"
    One stammered, "St-st-stand right there!"

A short, fat, cop reached
    for his waist to get some mace.
Stag took a drag then
    flicked his cig in his face.

The old cop faltered
    but a rookie felt bold,
thought he might slide up
    and try that old chokehold.

Wannabe Marine, still on that
    "Few Good Men" hype.
Stag cut a thin stripe straight
    across his windpipe.

More people gathered.
    Those on parole scattered.
Some carried banners
    reading "BLACK LIVES MATTER!"

YouTubers took video.
    Hippies chanted, "Peace!"
A few with fresh welts
    sang, "Fuck the Police!"

POP! POP! POP! RAT-
    TAT-TAT!!! in the air!
"Calling all cars,
    we need help over here!

We got a nigger cornered,
    far as we can see."
Dispatch asked,
    "Then what's the problem?"

Cop said, "His name is Stagolee!"

II.

Helicopter lights showered
    millions of cops,
armored trucks, snipers
    perched on tenement tops.

They shut down the block,
    barricades and yellow tape.
There seemed to be no way
    Stag could make his escape.

Stagolee hunkered down
    behind a brick wall
with his cell phone dying
    and nobody to call.

In his coat he had a flask,
    Desert Eagle, a few clips.
Half pack of Ports,
    one he flipped to his lips.

The standoff lasted
    well past the break of dawn.
The police chief reached
    for the captain's megaphone.

Said, "Stagolee, I'm tired
    and my patience is thin.
You got ten seconds, nigger,
    to turn your black ass in!"

Stag took a swig
    from his flask of gin,
And began to think
    what this country asks of men.

Stand here, go there.
    Don't be too big or too black.
He thought about the water hoses,
    police dog attacks.

He thought about Breonna
    Taylor, Emmett Till,
Oscar Grant at Fruitvale,
    Trayvon, and Sean Bell.

Sandra Bland, Rekia Boyd,
    George Floyd and Rodney King,
Freddie Gray, Shelly Frey. Long
    list, and that's the thing:

Stagolee knew they had
    no plans to let him walk.
He knew they had him measured
    for the bags and chalk.

Even innocent folk couldn't
    breathe and walk free.
He thought, "Let alone me,
    gangster ass Stagolee!"

He took another swig, dragged on
    his cig, then popped
a shot over the top of the wall
    and the boss cop dropped.

Bedlam and panic
    as the pigs ran frantic.
Stag kept blasting
    on some one man gang shit.

He unloaded, swore,
    then reloaded his .44,
lit up ten more,
    and the rest hit the floor.

Police pissed their pants
    up and down the boulevard.
S.W.A.T. team begged the mayor,
    "Call the National Guard!"

Days flew past. Tear gas,
    and now tanks.
To get Stagolee

the city broke the bank.

The President, too,
    sent Special Forces and Seals.
When asked, the Pope said, "By God,
    that nigga's just too real!"

Still. A Desert E clip
    only holds but so much.
And the soldiers wouldn't get
    close enough to touch.

Then the Assistant to the Assistant
    pulled the mayor aside
and said, "If you don't want him alive,
    think Philly in '85."

"You don't mean…
    EUREKA!" cried the mayor.
And before long
    a lone drone sliced the air.

Circled wide while the cops
    tried to clear the block,
then hovered, a hummingbird
    with the missiles cocked.

The mayor gave the gladiator sign,
    thumbs down.
The drone set its sights—
    then exploded mid-flight.

"Duck," the mayor screamed
    then scrammed, "Run for cover!"
Stagolee looked up
    and saw his number one lover

on the rooftop, leather

    bodysuit, a bazooka,
fro blowing in the wind.
    Stag said, "Awwwww, suki

suki, now!" She wasn't alone,
    she'd brought the Panther Brigade
singing, "Get up, Stand up."
    Stag knew he had it made.

She rode the zip-line in
    smooth to save the day.
Her name was Nikky Blakk
    from down Apopka way.

III.

Ladi dadi. Boy, Nikky Blakk
    sure had a body. The hotty
said, "Get ready," then
    tossed Stag a shotty,

12 gauge sawed off
    pistol grip, "Hold this."
Then she winked and blew
    Stagolee a gold-toothed kiss.

Now, I said I'd be quick,
    but here's where all gets good.
Nikky Blakk had gathered up
    all the boys in the hood,

homegirls with hand grenades,
    put pistoleros in place.
A Santero sang and killed
    a couple goats just in case.

They lit Pirellis on fire
    at each end of the street,

bottled gaseous rags flung
    at riot cops' feet.

Stag said, "I can last at least
    a dozen years, dozen days!"
That's when the president balked,
    said he had golf to play.

Ronald K. Chump
    left the mayor out to dry,
with his bullets run low
    and two tears in each eye.

The mayor cried, "Mr. President,
    Motherfucker, can't you see?!
I can't do it alone! That's
    that nigger, Stagolee!"

Then Chump said, "You're fired!
    Bigly! And I quit!"
Then signaled for his limo
    with the spoiler kit.

And while the president
    bickered with the mayor and cops,
one rebel snuck Stag and Nik
    a bag of props.

Nikky Blakk threw on a beard,
    tuxedo, and top hat.
Stag in drag, dress and wig,
    sashayed away out the back.

Stag chloroformed the driver,
    homies held down the goons,
Nikky Blakk phoned the Prez
    and said the car would come soon.

Chump saw the red bob wig
    and sequins on Stag's dress,
then hopped his ass right in
    and started groping for breasts.

He reached high and low
    to grab as much as he could,
and turned snow when Stag said,
    "Hey yo, Potna'! What's good?"

Chump had the bass in his face,
    a big ol' yam in his hand,
some chilly chrome to his dome,
    but still could not understand.

So Stagolee cleared his throat
    to run it down in a rant…
But Nikky Blakk shot the prez
    and was like, "I'm sorry, I can't."

They left the limo running
    with its presidential plates.
Nik said, "We can still catch *Shaft*,
    and Cheryl's is open late."

And by the time they found the limo
    with The Chump in the trunk,
Stag and Nik were back in Harlem,
    hugged up and half drunk.

Brian Batchelor

Political Arithmetic

A 5-gram crack rock
is the same weight
as the force needed
for gavel to crack
sounding board, meaning
it takes less than
a match tip's spark
struck by a judge & jury
of peers to ghost
a dealer or addict
to a mandate of
5 years minimum.

Let's crunch the numbers:
1 gram equals a pound
of flesh deboned,
the spine made abacus
Lady Justice fingers
arbitrarily. It's the dark
meat legislation finds most
savory, hunting every inner-
city dense with street-corners
until every subtracted son
and father fills
the state's bulging belly.

5 grams of what
puts a quick buck
in a hungry hand
is automatic imprisonment.

5 grams of what
makes the body choir itself

up from earth's hard ways
is automatic imprisonment.

A closed fist clutching
5 grams of nonviolence
is automatic imprisonment.

The war on drugs went wrong
when "war" was declared
the new political arithmetic
& the community minus
its black & brown men
became a battlefield with
the slaughtered removed.

Candace Williams

black, body

Antonin Scalia's WHREN v. UNITED STATES, 517 US. 806 (1996) decision rearranged in order of frequency, after Franny Choi

black body citizens civil compliance equal fear freedom good guarantees guise inconsistent inconvenient incriminating Justice light marijuana ship wiretap writ youthful race race respect respect traditional traditional faith faith faith opinion opinion opinion plainclothes plainclothes plainclothes valid valid validity illegal illegal illegal illegal occupants occupants occupants occupants ordinarily ordinary ordinary ordinary right right right right sped speed speed speeding unmarked unmarked unmarked unmarked view view viewed views constitutional constitutional constitutional constitutionality constitutionality drug drug drug drugs drugs followed followed following following following id id id id id interest interest interests interests interests inventory inventory inventory inventory inventory motivations motivations motive motive motive safety safety safety safety safety warrant warrant warrant warrant warrantless warrantless evidence evidence evidence evidence evidence evidence investigating investigation investigation investigation investigation investigatory issue issue issue issue issue issued purpose purpose purpose purpose purpose purposes fact fact fact fact fact facts facts standard standard standard standard standard standard standard intent intent intent intent intent intention intentionally intentions invalid invalid invalid invalidate invalidate invalidate invalidates invalidation mean meaning means means means means means means means order order order order ordinarily ordinary ordinary ordinary objective objective objective objective objective objective objectively objectively arrest arrest arrest arrest arrest arrest arrest arrestee arrested vehicle vehicle vehicle vehicle vehicle vehicle vehicle vehicles vehicles seizure seizure seizure seizure seizure seizure seizure seizures seizures seizures justifiable justifiable justification justification justification justified justifies justifies justify justify subjective subjective subjective subjective subjective subjective Subjective subjective subjectively subjectivity court court court court court court court court court court STATES States States States States States States States States States individual individual individual individual individual individual individual individual's individualized individuals individuals Fourth Fourth Fourth Fourth Fourth Fourth Fourth Fourth Fourth Fourth Fourth Fourth other other other other other other other other others otherwise otherwise See See See See see see see see see see See See law law law law law law law law lawful lawful lawfulness laws laws laws laws based based based based based based based based based bases basis basis basis basis basis basis pretext pretext pretext pretext pretext pretext pretext pretext pretext pretext pretext pretext pretexts pretextual pretextual pretextual violated violated violated violated violating violating violation violation violation violation violation violation violation violation violation violations violations violations reason reason reasons reasons reasons reasonable reasonable reasonable reasonable reasonable reasonable reasonable reasonable reasonable reasonableness reasonableness reasonableness reasonableness reasonably probable search search search search search search search search search search search search search search search searches searches searches searches searches stop stop stop stop stop stop stop stop stop stop stop stop stop stop stop stop stop stop stop stop stop we We We We we We We We we wewewewewe we we we we we we we we we we officer Officer officer officer Officer officer officer Officer officer officer officer officer officer officer officer officer officer officer officer officer Officer officer's officer's officer's officer's officer's officers officers

officers   officers   officers   police   police   police
police   police   police   police   police   Police   Police
Police   police   police   police   police   police   police
police   police   police   police   police   police
police   police   police   police   police   police

Hanif Abdurraqib

All the TV Shows Are about Cops

I crave, instead, the long shot
of the weary hustler at the blood-red doorway

between evening & night
reaching a hand for the cold metal

of a fridge that hums with its own
emptiness. yes, I have felt the sigh of the
cop

who goes to a comfortable house & dreams
of the forest, pulsing with branches bent

into what must look like gang signs
to someone with a racing heart & an eager

trigger. no, I will take the shot
of the hustler in a room lit

by a single lamp
I will take the shot from overhead

that tells us the hustler
is placing their stash in a box

or feeling, again, that merciful
weight of a gun with all its bullets
still tucked

like flower buds in the fist of a curious
child. if there is a way to get your paper

in america without knowing

that the getting of your paper might kill

you, then I don't want to know it
& my boys hustled cuz our parents

came home & sat in
driveways with the car engine
still on

like they were daring themselves
towards another, better highway

the shot I crave is the hustler
reaching into their pockets &

pulling out an entire block
worth of balled-up bills

someone's insurance money
that just came in but not for long

someone's college fund for the kid
who fixed their jump shot when the recruiters

came to town. a fistful of gentle thefts

I want the shot where the hustler pushes the money into another hand
& someone who loves them kisses the white ash from their knuckles.

Kenneth Nadeau

Everything I Know about Horses

And like when a fallen horse can't get up,
a nondescript vehicle comes to the rescue.
Shielding from ogling eyes, bang! Departing
vehicle leaves spectators baffled.

Everyone knows the cliches, "keep your head
up," "stay strong." It's code for, I don't
know what the fuck to say. Sometimes
words can't find meaning through a phone
on the other side of the plexiglass. Smiles,
tender eyes, blown kisses, slow the urge
to lay down in dung. "Horse shit," I
say when no words pass between us. What
can she say anyway when I'm facing
twenty-five to life

Summers I spent working at Suffolk Downs,
amongst the loan sharks, bookies and cadres
of young escorts. I served food and drinks
to connected attorneys with names like
Strefalino and Langone. I would scream,
"Come on, Come on," slapping the torqued
program against my thigh. As if the horse
I bet, would run faster. My voice drowned
in delirious cheers

Now I have no voice, hoarse from tears,
shed in county jail years ago. Fenced
in with other beasts, an existence of hay
and being rode until my legs break or
mind, in this race to nowhere

Losing sucks, I often did. But what about losing horses, ones that continually lost? Starved? Dehydrated? Already costing owners their life savings. Abandoned after short racing careers. Waiting on death in some far off neglected farm.

As I sit in my prison cell contemplating these facts, I now understand why, they just did as they were told.

IV

American Inferno: Inside the Cell

Leeann Parker

Free

I used to belong to the streets
taking problems however they came.
Searching for answers I see no
end to my pain.
Everyday it's the same thing.
I need to change my life
Now my life has caught up to me I am
Stuck in a place where there's
no relief.
Time stands still I'm losing
it as I speak.
Within these four walls if
They could speak,
They would tell a story of pain
and grief.
Pulled away from my kids when
They were five and nine,
Now they are growing up without
mommy by their side.
Never knew that my decisions
would catch up to me
Caged in chained down prison
has made me stronger.
I had to wrestle with my demons
for a little longer.
How can I ask the lord to spare me
just this one time.
When I know that in my heart
I should be crucified.

Evie Shockley

american inferno

the prison system is divine.
    a comedy of errors. funny
        how, like gods, we've carved
            out layer upon layer of *just*
        the right amount of hell
   for each offense, a downward
spiral from juvie to eternal
    life behind bars, from social
       and civic death to that lowest
          ring of fire, death row. like
       god, we act on wrath, insist
    there's a price to pay for
worshipping at the altar
    of greed or heedless pleasure,
       for disrespecting authority,
          insist that some must die
      in the wilderness without
   ever seeing the promise
of the land. no free bread
    dropping out of nowhere
       to fill the emptinesses. no
          beatrice to be or not to be.

Christopher Malec

Order's Up

Purpose is peripherally blind
swallowing planets whole
on Justice's smoke break

                                    where there's a happy hour
                                        the rest are busy cleaning toilets
                                  scrubbing ontology from under the rim

under the dim
a lot of wisdom applies for the job
advertised on the front of a consequence

                            no wonder the service is exceptionally fascist
                                  and takeout's almost encouraged
                              over a bar made from holding-cell benches

it's half-past sin
and I'm still waiting on my plate of resurrection to be served chilled
so I can wash it down with the worst kinda blasphemy mixed with my
best hypocrisy

                    taken; not earned

            but the only tips I'm giving are the ones I haven't learned
                            on an alley-way conveyor belt
                      piecing anarchies together one part at a time

otherwise they're wagered against my ponder
at how many games are gonna be watched
waiting to see if liberalism ever actually scores

                        the jukebox keeps playing in tune with the past
                no amount of quarters will allow you to skip the tracks

                                to a parking lot ballad of bruised success

as if on cue, one's bank heads directly into the corner's pocket
and on every rack the 8-ball's color is changing
to match the intention of the winning stick

                        the minutes keep clocking out by the second
                                so as soon as the moon's engulfed
                there'll be plenty of epistemology flushed down the drain

last calls for alcohol are communions for the destitute
take a seat, 'cause the guys rushing to the front
run the risk of tripping into a eulogy cover

or inner-city linked bracelets   maybe both

I've been waiting on my dish since exactly 8 happy hours ago

            and I agreed to refuse it's due to the extinction of common sense
                    or that I demand service from any cliche. . . like a prophet
                or that my waiter's break has persisted further than election day

a wait this long is gum stuck to the bottom of your dreams
while some jukeboxes just seem to get stuck on repeat
and the 8-ball keeps jumping back on the table before you can walk away

if it gets shaky, keep enough applications to shove under the leg
and hope this season ain't really started yet, so you can beat it
before those other tragedies start placing their bets

                    see I'm not looking for the whole lot; just a space
                                    or even a spot by the exit door
                        hoping next to it, and apron lays on the floor
                                                        a ticket within

says,
"resurrection to go" folded on top of the last two cigarettes turned up in
the box

Randall Horton

Flashback to the Cell

the last stop is also a beginning point
  on the C at 168th POETRY IS HARD
catches my eye before we depart
  against the reflecting neon signs
as square tiles parallel lives lived
  in a box or cell—we alone the man
& [I] of no significance until he exits—
  the grinding wheels pull away
from 155th—a ghost compartment now
  analogous to time spent in solitary.
i occupied this same mute hush
  when white boy met his living shadow
in a split second on the cold concrete
  bringing to view faces pressed
inside rectangle glass—the aftersound
  resonates loud year after year—
(white boy died from the epistles of dear john)
  appearing at 125th a person is reading
THE ESSENTIAL ETHERIDGE KNIGHT
  on the train today no one reads
& we continue swathed in noise—

Catherine LaFleur

Devour

I made this food. It's not much,
Ramen noodles, stolen chicken,
peanuts caramelized in Coke—
the real thing.

I stood two hours for the microwave.
Here, sit on your footlocker.
Use this pillow for your back.
Rest a minute.

Sliced pickles? Cheese?
I razor-bladed this apple
in the shape of
a lotus for you.

Relax, take off your shoes,
socks, and all that stress.
Taste, enjoy this prison
dinner fare.

Soon the night bird will sing
outside our cell window.

SHE > i

Cellfish

Too many sentences where I am the subject and (the) predicate.
One hundred eight months, being booked is a life deficit.
How in the pits, the bowels, the crevices… my shit has no precedence?

Paying your debt to society, a play on words—true vulgarity.
There is no rehabilitation, there is no redemption, no clarity.
My time was more than charity.

The days, the months, the years, for the State's prosperity.
High stakes in comparison—men versus women.
The wait has no gravity. Family plus sanity all weighs on your humanity.

Kennedy A. Gisege

Break from Madness

You shave your scalp then click
    your tongue like a boy who cuts

off his fuzz for the first time, snicks
    his chin as blood flows out, then stops

so madness can recede. Or does it,
    when you cut off your hand while

hacking up wood. Does madness
    begin to wane, then? Or when

the funeral drum rings with sinister
    distractions as a woman smiles at you?

Does madness flee for the he-bird
    when he warms eggs while the she-bird

goes to war? Because she-birds must do
    everything, not just dance when

the drum beats. How about when
    a singer yelps without notes and you

wonder if you are black enough or blue
    without being told madness is like that—

like waking up from a fever that says
    you need a break before it cuts, excoriates.

Eduardo Martinez

Cinderblock Calendars

i've been staring at the sun too long
stranded on a prison yard
flossing with barbed wire
spitting bars out like phlegm
stars orbiting my peripheral
young sons burning out with smoked lungs
assisted off a second hand no look pass
break the body
after the mind bends three ways like beach chairs
doing yoga in amphoras
fancy foot work around the phoenix's blinking cinders
'cause ain't no fire bird gon' be the death of me,
Desert Eagle for that green American eagle
'cause money ain't got no root grounded here,
seems somewhere we lost our ids in the ashes
and became numbers
we were Cassius Clay
before we went to prison and changed our names
and religion
took good looks at shook ones
American Gotham city gospel
batman gadgets and robbing will get you 25
crows fly with a sense of purge in their words
death is but a blind date flirting with release
3 strikes on a billy-club swing
hide and go seek
not sages but pages
"you want to hide something from a nigga,
put it in a book"
or keep them in cages it's a stand-up joke,
when 100,000 men talk about change
and don't nothing change
had chains on so long felt naked without the weight

these cells got low ceilings
keeping our reach limited
this encrypted script
been doing high fives with enemies
since the age of five
my feet learned early how to moon walk on ceilings
mixing gypsy tea leaves
with a Santeros coffee bean talk
if pediatricians were palm readers
we'd crush curses like garlic cloves
and suck the mercury like snake venom
out of children's vaccinations that might just prevent
a newborn baby from being autistic
or a 15-year-old
from spraying the chalk board burgundy with an AR-15
help! graffitied in crayon or outlined in asphalt chalk
in finger paint blood
kids are making snow angels in the ashtray
sun burned vision
soot colored point of views
were all shaded holy relics
animated statues having a bootleg Broadway
on a cemetery plot
in the parking lot
there's always a school bus flattened in the handicap spot
while hearses and ambulances have reserved parking
and it's hard to tell the difference
dancing from a distance
if the lot is a schoolhouse
a courthouse
or a prison
cause they all have fences, metal detectors, and police
how will the city ever make bail
when they valet kids
in a system
where freedom isn't cheap
x'd out in boxes. . . left forgotten
like old calendars on concrete

Natalie Diaz

Under Correction II

Last month I went to a new therapist for the first time.
Because my country is sick and I am my country's
valued customer and chronic patient. My sister is not treated
by doctors but by prison guards and bus drivers—

my sister is treated with diesel therapy.
They move her from facility to facility with no warning
or explanation. Because they can. I follow her, because I must.
I follow her into every television or video screen:

Vizio. Samsung. Panasonic. Sony. ICS. Securus. Global Tel Link.
I am learning a lot about television/video monitors.
I am learning so much about television/video monitors
that they will soon give me a degree.

I am becoming a professor of communications. I have a degree
of hatred in me. I am a knowledge system. I speak in code.
I have been in so many video screens that I know all the cells
in a plasma display are smashed together, held inside

by two glass plates—front/back. Like my sister, who is also held
inside, who is also smashed in a cell. We are someone's video
game. We are a reality TV show. We are *Survivor*. We are *Lost*.
I am a student of the price my sister pays and to whom she pays it:

> The Ford Foundation Justice Grant
> gave me money to write this poem, invested
> in me while simultaneously investing in
> the system which has imprisoned my sister
>
> in the television. The Ford Foundation gave me money
> and I use it. I use Ford's money to send my sister books,

to put money on her books so she can buy toothpaste
and ramen noodles she eats with a comb. I also use it

to buy time for phone calls, for video phone calls, anything
to get closer to my sister. The system takes the money
I pay them—my mother pays them, my brother pays them,
my sister's four kids pay them—to talk to my sister

and gives it back to the Ford Foundation in private
equity, so they can give it to the next sister who has a sister
who is serving time and needs to buy time on the phone.
It is an equitable process—equal opportunity for sisters

like me, like mine. We are especially lucrative
for the Ford Foundation. My three-year old niece
and four-year old nephew ask to talk to their mother
every morning and evening. Even when they cannot.

I am caught in the middle of a riddle of glass
because I came to prison and made the mistake of looking
for my sister who is held somewhere behind the glass,
from where I am held in the room behind the glass.

I'm glad you're here, she says, and I am not sure
what she means by *here*. It feels like we are both nowhere.
I go on letting my sister think we both are here—
smashed but at least together. I can't bear to correct her.

I won't say, *There are a thousand concrete blocks
and seven hundred years separating us*—(a basic blueprint
for a Nation or an arts institution). But these days I know less
about architecture and everything about video monitors.

For example: This screen has fingerprints smudged on it,
from other visitors who reached out to touch who was not there,
not really there. I tell myself, *Do not touch the screen, Natalie.
Do not let the guards see you wanting touch*—

do not let them know they are punishing your body
by taking your body away, by correcting your body
so that it remembers it does not deserve to touch its sister.
Do not reach out and touch the screen, do not audition

for this role, do not act this script—do not
remind your sister her body is being corrected to a condition.
I do not touch the screen. I cannot touch my sister.
I don't ask my sister if she's okay, but she tells me.

She says, *I'm okay*. But her words come out in cipher,
in all the old shapes—zigzags of water, the wind spiral,
a ram, a woman, a maze. And I know she means
There is no such thing as okay in here.

My sister needs money to buy a thermal. It's cold in her cell
and her blanket is worn thin. I tell her, *Maybe it's cold
to keep germs away, like at a hospital.* We both know it is so cold
because they know all the ways to punish my sister.

But this is their mistake, I think. This coldness. It is making
my sister remember her body. Her body is fighting
this punishment. It is shivering as if to say, *I deserve more.*
I am watching her shiver from outside or inside the television/

video monitor—I am in my mind, all this time, holding my sister
in my arms. I am waiting to use some of the Ford Justice Grant
to put money on my sister's books so she can buy a thermal.
And I will publish this poem to say thank you for the money.

Patricia Smith

Only One Clock

For the women of Bedford Correctional Center

I.

I'm sure I know the very moment when
the room became its walls, became the clawed,
unyielding door, became the backhand slap
of window, smeared opaque with merely all

their million breaths. I'd come with only words
arrayed in gusts of light, the hex I hoped
would daze the wary inmates for the hour
and disappear the latches on their lives.

The front of any room is such a scrubbed
and twitchy place, especially when I
am armed with just my thrashing passions while
an audience of strangers thinks me strange.

I'm calmed by other voices in the air.
But asked to share a thing about themselves,
not one revealed her joy or mused upon
a place that once was home. Instead they spoke

in clock—*Got 30 more of them in here*
or *Had to whup some ass, they added 5.*
One sniffed until I met her blaring eyes—
I just did 13 years, that's half the way.

The legendary one, who'd been unarmed,
had driven getaway in '81—
three people, two of them in blue, had bled
to gone. But now her shout commanded space:

How many years for me? The rest of them!
and all the women laughed, so I laughed too,
at first not realizing Julia meant
that she was in the place she'd always be,

and all the awkward cackling meant
she wouldn't be alone—the sisterhood
had vowed that every one of them would learn
to tend a spewing wound and mimic glee.

II.
When quiet dropped as if a whip had cracked,
they held my eyes—and their implicit dare
was red and human in the room. The gaunt
and haunted butch, who never stopped the drag

of fingers through her harshly scissored naps,
wanted to know if all my pretty lines
could resurrect the movement of a mouth
that knew her body long before its fall.

And then, a blue-black diva, petulant
and comically aloof—who looked as if
some horrid miscommunication had
resulted in her being plopped among

these filthy-mouthed, unkempt, much lesser class
of folk—insisted I unearth a rhyme
to finally twist the record back to right.
And Julia, who had driven murderers

away from what they'd killed, now owned the room
and saw no reason to renounce her reign.
Go on and read your poems now, she barked,
because you know enough about us, right?

Another inmate raised her hand and seemed
to want to speak, but then she dropped that hand
instead to veil a ruined mouth. Her back
was bended almost twice—I think she knew

that it would only straighten when she died,
and that she'd die right there in Bedford with
her mourners squalling from a single throat.
Her whole collapsing body was the time,

and any poem I could write for her
would just have kept on ending. *Listen now,*
I said, *I'll read you what I have.* But all
the lines were this: *I cannot shatter clocks.*

III.

The line was this: *i cannot shatter clocks*
and in the middle of that line, somewhere
inside the real of that, a woman screamed

and screamed. She wasn't in the room with us—
I thought that she was down a hallway, far
enough away—her screaming shouldn't have rocked

our walls the way it did. But no one seemed
to notice. No one raised their head or looked
in the direction of the door. There were

no startled glances, quizzical, alarmed,
all during the time the woman failed to pull
in any breaths, or bellow just one word

that I could understand. I scanned the room,
and thought of running down the hall myself
to see if I could help, but all I had

were poems—and I didn't want to see
her anguished face, or all the blood I knew
she must be drowning in. *What's happening?*

I asked. *What's going on? Should we get out?*
The woman who was halfway done at 13 years
had pity finally, and simply said

We can't go home. Until we've done our time—
for some of us, until we die—we can't
go home. No matter what has happened there,

we have to hear it here and tough it out.
And then I knew that they had understood
the words the screaming woman buried deep.

You've got to let me out, my mama's dead.

Each time she hurt the air, they heard the clock.

V.

What Is Caged Is Also Kept from Us: The People

Vicki Hicks

The First Day

Handcuffed in a dog box
Pull up in the Sally Port
not sure what to expect
"Keep your hands behind your back"
Walk up to a window
"What is your social?"
Coldly I recite it
To the showers next
Ice cold; no pressure
Hard towel to dry off with
"Squat cough; do it again"
My new wardrobe
Navy dress and crocs
"Your hair is dripping"
Use my dress to mop it up
Sitting in a cage like an animal
Cut my nails with used clippers
Take a picture
Document my tattoos
List my relatives
urine test
blood work
All on the First day!

Patricia Smith

But the Phone Rings Sometimes

I.
I have to decide to answer the phone. When I click
to pick up, this is the way it goes. There's that blip
of echoed air and I say *hello, hello?* before his new
mama, disembodied white female middle American

all-purpose monotone, informs me I have a collect call
from an inmate of the Middlesex House of Corrections.
And in the silence left open for his name, my son barks
Damon! gravel and guttural and studied badass, and *oh,*

I realize, blindwalking into what now passes for ritual,
it's just my son again, his cage gracelessly unlatched
so that he can mumble, temporarily reach into other air.
And tell me that his cellmate plans to kill him in his sleep.

Then I'm just another drooped mama in a ceaseless
snaking line, summoning my cinematic coo (lately, it
seems, the child is always, always about to be murdered).
Only seconds later, I'm being treated to a blow-by-blow

chronicle of the shaving of his head, and the sloppy gouge
when the distracted barber's razor dug deep, and *mama,
ha, ha, there was blood everywhere, but it look all right
now. Wait till you see, I'm baldheaded!* In the next breath,

I'm scared. Mama, I'm sick. I cough all night. Then, as
if he hadn't just swift-whispered that weakness, he shifts
to a sputter of jailhouse legalese, bringing me up to date
on his creaky version of hope—*since I never been in jail*

before and since I been staying out of trouble in here

*and since I been doing everything they say and since it
wasn't my gun...* But does it matter what grace the system
grants, if he's eating well or wrong, if the sentences run

together or top of one another, if he's crazy about his
mama? Because when dark drops and my son can no
longer fight sleep, a man, savagely focused, will arc
over him, hefting a sock swollen with dead D batteries.

Again. Because of the dozens of times he swears it's
about to happen, I've become an expert at visioning my
son's already nicked skull collapsing and slick with itself.
Two hundred miles away, I wince, gamely wear his wound.

II.

There's a picture of Damon, snapped over 20 years ago
when he was 2. It's black and white, just one unkempt
moment in the life of a kid, a snap only a mother craving
an unburdened memory could love. His gray sweatsuit

is caked with grime, his crown impossibly kinked. Staring
at the photo, I long to plunge my hands into those raucous
naps, kiss his nose and scoop his resisting wriggle
into my arms to snort that rusty meld of sugar and funk.

A voice interrupts. *Ma, Ma?*
It is twenty years later again.
I should have never picked up the phone.

III.

I can get in my car and drive toward him, filling three
highway hours with Motown's begging men, brown liquor
Aretha songs, and those damned insistent pictures of my
boy the way he used to be—deadpan jokester, giggling

gumcracker, stupefied by rockets and girls. Then, without
mercy, he sprouts upward, dons cavernous denims, stows
away screw-top wine and morphs into OG, cocked cannon,
baby maker, rhymebuster, lemming, lemming, lemming.

The last picture, the one of him I hate the most, stays with
me the longest—there's the grasping whiner who *really*
needs canteen money but never thanks me for raising his
four-year-old daughter. He's the single-syllable grunt, head

scarred, grossly swollen from prison workouts, who I
avoid mentioning to friends whose sons are waving grad
school acceptance letters or touring France with their jazz
bands. The most I will let on: *He's in Boston, on his own.*

I don't say: *He's locked up, but the phone rings sometimes.*

IV.
The waiting rooms are always too hot. I don't lift my eyes
often, but when I do, I see faces that mirror my own. Our
whole bodies sigh and sigh. We are in sweatshirts and jeans,
graying hair pulled back, eyes straight ahead, waiting for

our sons on the fresh-air side of bulletproof glass. A buzzer
sounds and a door slides open for their strained parade.
They shuffle as if shackled by boredom, plump and sinew
swathed in jumpsuits the color of storm. They are missing

molars, sudden bellies, downcast gaze, gang love scorched
into biceps. Numbed and innocent, numbed and guilty,
they stream in, scanning the drab room for mama or bae
or m'dear or maybe somebody, anybody, from the block,

somebody who remembers them free. Like toddlers, they
hug awkwardly, check out who else has come to see
who else, slyly size up their tribe, and greedily eye

the vending machines, broken and bulging with poisons.

I scour faces, wonder if my son's homicidal cellmate has allowed him dawn. And then there he is. Damon, damn him, serves up that grin, guaranteed to slap my heart open. He sputters a few words, *See how big my arms are getting?*,

then shuts to a silence, waiting for mama to come through, mutter a flimsy bandage, make it all better. Looking down the long, sorrowful row, I see that expectant hush repeated, repeated. All those mothers wanting desperately to be there

but wishing they hadn't come. If only we'd stayed home, listening to the phone ring and ring and not picking up. We could just keep staring out of our own jails into an unbending dark, wallowing in blue, waiting for the son to rise.

Ada Limón

What Is Caged Is Also Kept from Us

They come back to you as a sign
when someone dies, they say, a dragonfly,

some dull moth skimming a mud puddle,
a hummingbird in the ditch's golden rod.

But what if they are alive? But not allowed
to live? How do they return, then? Cricket

under the sink for three nights straight.
Why do we call it a song? That scraping

that needy stridulation. Scraper to file,
file to scraper. One song is for calling,

another to scare away, but they all sound
the same in the ghost hours of emptiness.

He does not come back. And she? She
does not see him in the red bird's black

mask or the dreary pinks of another dusk.
He is no symbol, no easy animal omen.

She opens the window to fetch only air.
He does not even have a window to open.

Reginald Dwayne Betts

When Every Word Is a Name

We waited without a name,
For your wonder, & after
You entered this world, wailing
Like the dragons, your tiny
Hands reaching for light
At the hour of the jumbo jet,
We waited & three days passed
Without words to announce this
Gift, & I read poems to myself,
& didn't think of the compass
I'd give you, years later, or
The compass you'd become
For me, & that evening, for
The first time, I was not lost,
Just discovering a story to tell
Myself about your curious eyes,
Aren't we always looking for a story
To tell ourselves? Isn't a name just
Shorthand for a myth? We gave
You a word in two tongues,
The English a translation
For the Hebrew, or vice versa,
Each the name of your mother's
Older brother — the uncle you'll
Never meet, the names pulled
From the Book, some wonder,
When I held you, your little body
Was neither wail nor howl, but
so fragile, & unafraid of these
Shivering hands or the warm
Water I used to bathe you — you,
Light from your mother's belly,
Patient, & smiling then, as if

You knew, you were the first
Song to find me worthy.

Jessica Hill

Reasons

When I speak, my words are immediate.
They pierce the ears, widen the eyes
and shock the heart.
So I write to lessen the impact of demons
in the dark.

I write to right the wrongs my hands have
done, to mourn my losses and celebrate
the battles I've won.

I write to discredit the naysayers
to edit the lies I've been holding.
To cut the bullshit and realize the dreams
I dream of unfolding

I write to shed light on misunderstood
dark skin.
To show the world that "different" isn't
a curse, a mistake, a sin.

I write to dance, to breathe, to laugh out loud,
to hope, to pray, to stand out in a crowd

I write with a pen, a pencil or a tiny piece of chalk,
I write to speak well
To put Boss in my walk.

I write.

Sin à Tes Souhaits

Sometimes I Wonder If God Really Fuck with Me Like That

& i mean if She don't who could really blame her my prayers
are hardly coherent hardly consistent too many drunk texts
too many requests for someone who don't call too much
i run out of words for God & i can't speak to my demons but
i hear them my language is never as big as my sins my grace
my demands which have taken to lingering in the back of my throat

& who can say whether God has favorites remembers only some
of our birthdays maybe She's exhausted maybe She's a simulation
i never know what's real i never know what to believe i used to
believe all i could have was the winter streets i kept returning to
fades funerals & the familiar cold of County & now i've made a home
in uncertainty my life is open concept i let the light wash through undesigned
warm enough to murk up the mirrors i am mostly alone & mostly unafraid
like a hummingbird at dawn September flowers are pinking in my yard

& on my father's gravestone too i sense a revolution & many dead
before spring ancestors way past impatient embracing their kin the sky
was my lover we laid all day with each other tried to figure out how
we could survive solo just the two of us & i don't know about you but
i can't say what any of this shit means i know how to make a poem
make a thing pretty & so must God but i've been so ugly & so has She

& i swore when i wrote this poem it would be all gold & saffron
thought it would smell like some pine forest epiphany at least
some cocoa butter at least an explanation but these are just words
& i'm not sayin i don't believe in God i'm just sayin She ain't easy
to read She don't respond She don't keep her read receipts on
i'm sayin my cousin still can't come home & my homie still can't come out
& yesterday i ate lamb & licked the blood from the plate & laughed
for an hour & everything was perfect & it feels like a trick

Evie Shockley

can't unsee

the eye is a tool. it takes
available light and makes notes

to self about shape, distance,
mood. the self—brain? mind?

soul?—accumulates and cross-
references these observations

with info from the ear, the skin,
the tongue, turns the memos

into memories we trust to be
true. what looks like wood

will not give beneath our feet.
what sounds like a siren

gives cause for alarm, will
be followed by flashing reds

and blues, or flames, or
a stretcher and a gun. the eye

is the open drawer of a file
cabinet the size of your head,

on the outside, and the size
of your life on the inside.

what goes in might get
lost, but never goes away.

if beale street could talk, jenkins
says baldwin says, it would say

soft sunshine sweater melting
chocolate. would whisper artist's

inner eye sends notes to hands
about shapes, distances, moods.

would speak on woman spine,
shout about black silence

and eloquent vocal black eyes.
jenkins' *beale street* says see?

the glow fonny's eyes emit
when tish is in view, the ideas

spinning and shifting behind
them when he studies his strange

sculpture-in-progress. see tish
discern that glow through prison

plexiglass, still smoldering through
a gray wash of gray. she can't

unsee the lips she kissed, even
when the mauve is bashed black-

blue—and she can't unsee
the bruise. meanwhile, fonny's

eyes are busily imprinting on his
psyche brutal scenes that befog

her face, that twist and disfigure
the structures he sculpts in his

    dreams. his visions always black
    & white, even when they're in color.

you can't unkill. and you can't
unjail. the constitution doesn't

yet confer on us the right to not
have to think about this shit. we

thumbs-up a criminal justice system
with cold-blooded murderers in

mind, not the system we'd like
ourselves or our kin to fall into.

have you ever made a mistake?
has a witness ever? an officer?

a jury? a judge? when we think
violent crime, if we see black

skin, history's whispering its old
lies into our colorblind ears,

making it easier for us to say *better*
that i'm safe and the criminal's sorry

than to waste time uttering the word
alleged. you can't unsee slavery.

a woman is innocent until proven
angry. a man is innocent until

he fits the profile. a child is
innocent until she sees her mother

or father in cuffs. can't unsee. set
bail too high and in two weeks

we've upped the odds that a petty
thief becomes a well-connected

felon with even more reasons
to steal. i can't unsee the video

of the school security cop slamming
an african american girl, a student,

to the ground. no, not the north
carolina one, the south carolina

one. no, in texas the girl is latina,
and i can't unsee her abuse either.

>   race is a tool. the law is a tool.
>   they take power and make
>
>   inhumane order out of human
>   chaos. they make floors that will
>
>   not give beneath a brown girl's
>   skull. they make officers see black
>
>   and think gun. what sounds
>   alarming will be followed by cell
>
>   phone photos and video clips,
>   seens that yet another century's
>
>   minds and spirits will file away.

Cody Bruce

Identity of a Prisoner

The darkness in me
Wants to come out
To play, to destroy
I wish
There was no light left
To heal
To love
One day
I will be completely
Empty
One day
I can hate
I wish I could dig
my fingers into my face
And peel off this stupid skin
Expose everything that
I truly am
Nothing
I swallow bleach to
Cleanse my taint
To fade my blackened soul
As if I ever had one
I need to scar every
Inch of my body
So that everyone knows
To stay
Away
I am a hopeless ruin
That is what they say.

James Pearl

My Father the Sahib

Born Charles James Gaines in Georgia 1917.
His shoulders were broad around his neck.
With calloused and cracked hands he split
the air with his axe; gashing into the flesh of the
tree. Blow by blow sweat ran down the nape
of his shoe black skin.
Cheekbones sharp on his face like his Indian ancestors.
Hair like wool. Eyes black like the ravens in the cornfield.
From the moonlight; he hid his brother
in a casket: From
Jim Crow. Eyes filled with hate, peering from
the white cloak on his head.
Carrying flames in his hand.
At his typewriter he wrote his sermons.
His faith in God was strong. Armed with the
sword of the Bible. "He feared no evil."
He loved but it was rarely with a hug.
He was my adversary my protector!
He was the man I loved! I hated!
His brawn no longer carried the weight of his life.
He needed to go away and sleep.
I needed him to stay.

Gustavo Guerra

Vacillating

What I remember most was how happy
I was to see you; how I ran into
your denim-clad arms yelling "Papi!"
how it still echoes across time. We stood
bathed in a pool of golden light from the porch,
the same porch where I would take pictures
in a Spiderman costume, just a few months
later crouched on hands and feet. Mom
came out and you began to argue, back
and forth, about you taking me out and
her already having plans. She grabbed my legs
and pulled, but you would not let go.
Back. And. Forth. Before my next birthday,
my third, you pulled the trigger and left me
forever. I can't help think you a coward for
leaving me to experience the malice of a stepfather's
words, to feel the force of his calloused hands,
to face life without a father's love. Then again,
I think I am a coward for not following in your
footsteps and ending the misery of my life
sentence the same way. I can't decide.

Sarah Lynn Maatsch

Click!

Click!
Transgender clinic closes do.. Click!
Trans youth denied treatmen.. Click!
Parent medical choices restri.. Click!
Are you awake yet?.. Click!
Trans girls can't play sports a.. Click!
Governor targets trans health.. Click!
Prison time for opposite gen.. Click!
An eye languors a moment closed
I was never asleep, only resting
Click!
Open to the third and truth strips bare
Fear sleeps with ignorance and breeds insanity
Click!
Blindfolds slither away and thoughts grow teeth
Are you afraid yet?
Click!
But blindfolds were never needed
They'd already been blinded
Click!
Strength uncoils at the sound of trumpets
Turtle shells were always a trick
Click!
A sea of voices crests, unified
A prismatic shield stands against the gavel
We lose everything, nothing left to fear
Click!
Lawmakers squeeze for juice
But rocks bleed nothing
Are you ready yet?
Click! And you'll miss it. . .

Angel Nafis

Ghazal to Open Cages

> *"We'll still live with the outside,*
>   *with its people and animals, struggle and wind—"*
>   —Nâzım Hikmet

If my trifling mouth might I call you brother. Might travel—creaky bitten,
black; the phone line of a poem will show how.

Relentless teacher. Ghost I choose. No parent, no province,
no palm can erase you. What fire's afraid of its own glow? How?

Beneath bloom, beneath wing, under a God-shucked sky,
your freedom is a fragrance even below How.

O, I must close my eyes to say this brother, but: the breast, the
heat, & long rain of a woman will find you no how.

Rippling brain, harvest of the captive, make a way out of none.
When I say a universe thrums in there do not go: how?

If filth rises above floorboards. If steel knows you like the pit knows
the plum. Be the song. The Crow. The How.

How could we love you right but fasten no roses to your name? Your
spirit, your heart—a frayed reed that knows how.

Nâzım, show us a room dying can't enter. Past grave & flesh. They
clog the river's flow? They imprisoned a poet? How?

VI.
The Nakedness Dark Demands: Surveillance and Shapeshifting

Vanessa Angélica Villarreal

Architect 3

1776. The birth of the United
States is inextricable from the birth
of the prison with the construction
of Walnut Street Jail, built to relieve
overcrowding and inhumane
conditions at Old Stone Jail.

Men, women, and children
are confined together in common
cells and subjected to public
whipping or branding. Illness is
rampant. Experimental isolation
and labor begin.

America, the story you tell
begins in the red glare of revolution,
freedom from empire and taxes,
but never with your revolutionary
brutality, driving innovation.

1787. What will become the prison
begins in Philadelphia, in the mind
of Benjamin Franklin.
At the Philadelphia Society
for Alleviating the Miseries
of Public Prisons, a group
imagines solitary confinement
and labor to encourage penitence
and reflection.

First American, inventor of the lightning
rod and bifocals, you also imagined
the modern penitentiary as a Quaker

monastery, and the unbearable enforced
silence of solitary confinement. The trick
of the Enlightenment is how its sciences
rationalize atrocities in the colonies, but
will be praised for the modern marvel
of the architecture.

1829. Eastern State Penitentiary
opens and receives its first inmate,
Charles Williams, Burglar.
Light Black Skin. Farmer by trade.
Can read. Sentenced to two years
segregated confinement with labor.

Would he be anything other than Black?
America's first penitentiary inmate: a Black
farmer who stole a watch, a coin, and a key.
The three things stolen from the enslaved:
time, compensation for labor, freedom.

The Pennsylvania System:
23 hours a day of complete solitude
and silence, prisoners are not allowed
to speak or see any inmates. Prisoners
do low-wage labor such as shoe-making.
Movement out of the cell requires a hood
to maintain anonymity and isolation.

[Listen: the earth is tense with memory,
each tree a nerve recording the history
that will defeat history. A gem of coal
is a demon, a boll of cotton, a reed of sugar cane,
a tumor of gold. Blue behind a gun.
The gridwork that holds bodies. We will
begin again with a riot of heat to stay alive.]

Kalief, I can think only of you. The
two years in isolation you survived

Figure 1. *Eastern State Penitentiary on Cherry Hill, 1856.*

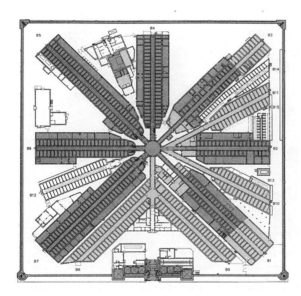

Figure 2. *Radial Plan, from Eastern State Penitentiary Historic Site.*

PART VI: THE NAKEDNESS DARK DEMANDS | **123**

echoed in the two years of the first
prisoner in the United States, also in
isolation. The excruciating silences
around you, the excruciating silence
you left behind, the silence of power,
and everything we could not
change.

1836. Eastern State Penitentiary
is completed on eleven acres, with
recreation yards and centrally heated
cells with arched ceilings, skylights,
and plumbing. It becomes the
model for prisons around the world, and
a tourist attraction.

1877. Four new cell blocks are built
between existing ones. No recreation
yards.

1911. Cell block 12, three stories, 120 cells,
is built wedged between the radial
wings, meant to hold three times
as many prisoners. The concrete cells
have one small window. By 1926, all
outdoor space is replaced with 3-story cell blocks.

1933-34. Prisoners riot over lack
of recreational space, low wages,
and overcrowding. Idleness
exacerbates mental illness.

1961. Cells are desegregated.

[Listen: the earth is tense with memory,
each tree a nerve recording the history that will defeat history. A gem
of coal emerges a diamond, a boll of cotton, a reed of sugar cane, a
tower of gold. Blue behold blue. The grid of redwood roots.
We will begin again, alive.]

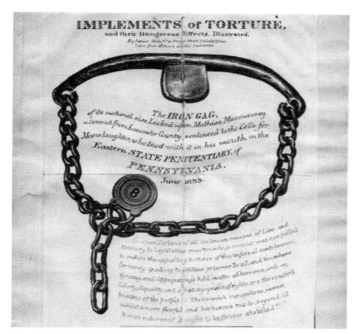

Figure 3: *The Iron Gag, used to enforce silence and prevent prisoners from talking.*

Figure 3a: *The gag is fitted over the prisoner's tongue and locked, pinning the prisoner's arms behind their back. In 1833, prisoner Mathias Maccumsey died from the device.*

Parole Denial Reason #1 (Dropdown)	Parole Denial Reason #2 (Dropdown)	Parole Denial Reason #3	Parole Denial Reason #4
Parent Does Not Wish to Separate	Flight Risk	Final Order/Pending Removal	In America, the land is the ghost of the land
Parent Does Not Wish to Separate	Flight Risk	Final Order/Pending Removal	In America, the land is the land of the ghost
Parent Does Not Wish to Separate	Flight Risk	Final Order/Pending Removal	In America, the land of the ghost in the land
Parent Does Not Wish to Separate	Flight Risk	Final Order/Pending Removal	In America, the land is the ghost
Parent Does Not Wish to Separate	Flight Risk	Final Order/Pending Removal	In America, the ghost is the land
Parent Does Not Wish to Separate	Flight Risk	Final Order/Pending Removal	inam
Parent Does Not Wish to Separate	Flight Risk	Final Order/Pending Removal	er ica th e
Parent Does Not Wish to Separate	Flight Risk	Final Order/Pending Removal	land of the
Parent Does Not Wish to Separate	Flight Risk	Final Order/Pending Removal	[is the]
Parent Does Not Wish to Separate	Flight Risk	Final Order/Pending Removal	ghost land
Parent Does Not Wish to Separate	Flight Risk	USCIS/IJ Review	the border becomes a site of spatial-temporal
Parent Does Not Wish to Separate	Flight Risk	USCIS/IJ Review	inequality, where first world nations extract
Parent Does Not Wish to Separate	Flight Risk	USCIS/IJ Review	time and lifespans
Parent Does Not Wish to Separate	Flight Risk	Final Order/Pending Removal	from the nations south of the US/Mexico border,
Parent Does Not Wish to Separate	Flight Risk	Final Order/Pending Removal	the line itself manufactures temporal-social-spatial inequality
Parent Does Not Wish to Separate	Flight Risk	Final Order/Pending Removal	and corrupts the archive
Parent Does Not Wish to Separate	Flight Risk	Final Order/Pending Removal	creating slippages of time that manifest
Parent Does Not Wish to Separate	Flight Risk	Final Order/Pending Removal	as those who remember from those who don't
Parent Does Not Wish to Separate	Flight Risk	Final Order/Pending Removal	those who belong to the past
Parent Does Not Wish to Separate	Flight Risk	USCIS/IJ Review	and those who belong to the future
Parent Does Not Wish to Separate	Flight Risk	USCIS/IJ Review	dividing languages, histories, families, futures
Parent Does Not Wish to Separate	Flight Risk	Final Order/Pending Removal	
Parent Does Not Wish to Separate	Flight Risk	Final Order/Pending Removal	Western temporal-spatial domination
Parent Does Not Wish to Separate	Flight Risk	Final Order/Pending Removal	thrives on forgetting and displacement
Parent Does Not Wish to Separate	Flight Risk	Final Order/Pending Removal	
Parent Does Not Wish to Separate	Flight Risk	Final Order/Pending Removal	Migration is an act inextricably bound to childhood
Parent Does Not Wish to Separate	Flight Risk	Final Order/Pending Removal	the wolf womb, the open portal, the time-wound.
Parent Does Not Wish to Separate	Flight Risk	Final Order/Pending Removal	the dark pines shining back eyes,
Parent Does Not Wish to Separate	Flight Risk	Final Order/Pending Removal	the shineback,
Parent Does Not Wish to Separate	Flight Risk	Final Order/Pending Removal	the crying woman
Parent Does Not Wish to Separate	Flight Risk	Final Order/Pending Removal	the slap from a man
Parent Does Not Wish to Separate	Flight Risk	Final Order/Pending Removal	the slap back
Parent Does Not Wish to Separate	Flight Risk	Final Order/Pending Removal	the hole in the wall
Parent Does Not Wish to Separate	Flight Risk	Final Order/Pending Removal	the fist in the girl
Parent Does Not Wish to Separate	Flight Risk	Final Order/Pending Removal	the half-moon split between nations
Parent Does Not Wish to Separate	Flight Risk	Final Order/Pending Removal	the obliterated nation
Parent Does Not Wish to Separate	Flight Risk	Final Order/Pending Removal	the chord in the bedroom
Parent Does Not Wish to Separate	Flight Risk	Final Order/Pending Removal	the milky flame
Parent Does Not Wish to Separate	Flight Risk	Final Order/Pending Removal	the leaf of cloth around the child
Parent Does Not Wish to Separate	Flight Risk	Final Order/Pending Removal	the found secret
Parent Does Not Wish to Separate	Flight Risk	Final Order/Pending Removal	the way down
Parent Does Not Wish to Separate	Flight Risk	Final Order/Pending Removal	
Parent Does Not Wish to Separate	Flight Risk	Final Order/Pending Removal	the migrant child is the figure that *motivates* the abject cruelty
Parent Does Not Wish to Separate	Flight Risk	Final Order/Pending Removal	of white supremacist violence
Parent Does Not Wish to Separate	Flight Risk	Final Order/Pending Removal	Children represent the future
Parent Does Not Wish to Separate	Flight Risk	Final Order/Pending Removal	and migrant children are the embodiment
Parent Does Not Wish to Separate	Flight Risk	Final Order/Pending Removal	of what drives white racial anxiety
Parent Does Not Wish to Separate	Flight Risk	Final Order/Pending Removal	a future in which whites
Parent Does Not Wish to Separate	Flight Risk	Final Order/Pending Removal	are outnumbered and replaced by non-white migrants
Parent Does Not Wish to Separate	Flight Risk	Final Order/Pending Removal	and their children
Parent Does Not Wish to Separate	Flight Risk	Final Order/Pending Removal	
Parent Does Not Wish to Separate	Flight Risk	Final Order/Pending Removal	The child in the image is no longer a human being but a debate
Parent Does Not Wish to Separate	Flight Risk	Final Order/Pending Removal	a symbol flattened by rhetoric
Parent Does Not Wish to Separate	Flight Risk	Final Order/Pending Removal	her grief and terror on loop
Parent Does Not Wish to Separate	Flight Risk	Final Order/Pending Removal	dimming before our very eyes
Parent Does Not Wish to Separate	Flight Risk	Final Order/Pending Removal	
Parent Does Not Wish to Separate	Flight Risk	Final Order/Pending Removal	
Parent Does Not Wish to Separate	Flight Risk	Final Order/Pending Removal	
Parent Does Not Wish to Separate	Flight Risk	Final Order/Pending Removal	
Parent Does Not Wish to Separate	Flight Risk	Final Order/Pending Removal	
Parent Does Not Wish to Separate	Flight Risk	Final Order/Pending Removal	
Parent Does Not Wish to Separate	Flight Risk	Final Order/Pending Removal	
Parent Does Not Wish to Separate	Flight Risk	Final Order/Pending Removal	
Parent Does Not Wish to Separate	Flight Risk	Final Order/Pending Removal	
Parent Does Not Wish to Separate	Flight Risk	Final Order/Pending Removal	
Parent Does Not Wish to Separate	Flight Risk	Final Order/Pending Removal	
Parent Does Not Wish to Separate	Flight Risk	Final Order/Pending Removal	
Parent Does Not Wish to Separate	Flight Risk	Final Order/Pending Removal	
Parent Does Not Wish to Separate	Flight Risk	Final Order/Pending Removal	
Parent Does Not Wish to Separate	Flight Risk	Final Order/Pending Removal	

Patrick Rosal

An excerpt from "Notes from the Visitations," a work in progress

Apo…

Apo!!!!!!

Apo?

El que quiera ver algún demonio debe rezar el Credo al dar las ocho de la noche y al pronunciar la resurrección de la carne, incline su cabeza hasta casi tocar la tierra y verá entre sus pies la mar de espíritus malignos.

—Isabelo de los Reyes y Florentino. *El Folk-lore Filipino (Tomo I)*

Twenty years ago all the Filipinos in the United States could have been comfortably fitted into your suite of rooms Mr. Chairman…Today there are approximately 60,000 Filipinos in the United States. Of that number 50,000 are in the State of California. Only 4 percent of the entire number of Filipinos in the United States are female. If you assume that those females are married into their own race, it will leave 46,000 unattached, unmarried, young Filipinos in this country whose ages range between 17 and 25. Imagine an army of 46,000 troops, approximately 40 regiment, 46,000 Filipinos from the ages 17 to 25 in mass formation.

—from Statement of Honorable R.J. Welch, Representative in Congress from the State of California, Hearings Before the Committee on Immigration and Naturalization, Seventy-First Congress, Second Session on H.R. 8708

Además de los anitos de ambos sexos y los animales venerados, los ilocanos han tributado, si no culto verdadero, cierto respeto á los objetos muy útiles. Los campesinos ilocanos dan el tratamiento de Apo (señor) al oro, plata, dinero, arroz, sal, la tierra y todo lo muy útil en general…llegó un tiempo en que todo sobre la tierra fue Dios, excepto el verdadero Dios.

—Isabelo de los Reyes y Florentino.

Is someone there?

Yes
Someone

Is someone whistling?
Someone is singing

Is someone dancing?
They are
They are dancing

And him
What's he doing there?
Is he crying?

He is looking

He is looking at his hands

      *

legend:incomplete

Philadelphia, PA; Watsonville, CA; Edison, NJ; Delano, CA; Morgan Hill, CA; Manila, Philippines; Madrid, Spain; Bioko, Equatorial, New Guinea; Laoag, Philippines; Vigan, Philippines; San Vicente, Philippines; Caoayan, Philippines; Batac, Philippines; Toronto, Canada; Brooklyn, NY; Jersey City, NJ; Pahoa, Hawaii; Kalihi, Honolulu, Hawaii; Chicago, Illinois

I've been holding off on telling this
                              to you.
I can't tell if it's a lie or not.   A dream
         or a vision

                  Or fact.

I don't even know where to begin
                I wonder if I'm going crazy
But some days I sit here in my own apartment
         and I could just   go
without my legs   twenty years
fifty   a hundred years   I can go
         . . .   I'm saying   . . .
         I've spent these days learning
how to travel in time
         I've practiced being a ghost
I can visit the dead.   And I thought maybe
it would be like   just sitting down
and asking questions and they would talk back to me
         but even if you could find them in their rooms
sometimes they don't see you.   Most times
they don't see you.   It's not good
         to learn how to do this
When you step into your ghost body   you can't
      take people with you.   You can't
take the living with you.   You have to go alone.
                  And then when you come back

*Es malo silbar
por la noche,
porque acuden
fantasmas.*

—Isabelo de
los Reyes y
Florentino

no one's going to believe that you were there
    There's nothing physical that you can bring.
There's nothing that you can carry.   Nothing
you can film   or record   There's no physical evidence.
    I want to tell the
things that I've seen.
I want to tell you the people   I've seen.

But I can't   promise you   that I know them.
I can't promise you that   I have solved their mysteries

any better than   they have   I can't promise you
that I've solved even my own.   I don't even know why
    I started to do this.

El verbo escuchar significa entre la gente de Manila mirar por un agujero.
—de los Reyes y Florentino

    Sometimes the dead call me.

They never ask me to write anything down.
They're not even sure they want to tell me their story.
    I don't even have a whole story to give you.
I can only tell you what I saw   which is incomplete
    which is full of incredible wonder   and sadness
    Out of the hundreds of millions of souls in the past

I don't know why   I was called by the ones who called
me.

Some of them are my family.   Some of them
are absolute strangers.   I don't even know

if they're telling the truth.   And I don't expect you to
believe everything.   I'm not sure I do either.

I'm not even sure who gave me this job. But I know this—

I can't keep going back
         and not tell anybody what I've seen
     even if no one wants to listen.

*

I have to tell you about a man making a kite first. And I don't know the whole story of the kite but I see him now, pinching a stick to a folded corner of newspaper. He's sitting in a chair. He's a young man. (This I know is one of the facts.) But if I turn away and then look again, it turns out he's an old man.

No one bothers to make a kite any more. But this man, who must be around 22, has taken some newsprint and folded it, over the edge of a scuffed up table to tear the sheet clean.

I'm speaking to you from this room—his room, though he shares it. The place is dark, lit by a couple kerosene lamps. It is 1929. This isn't a lie. We are just east of Monterey, the water, the bay, and its terrific, deadly lace breaking over the sand. Maybe you've stood on that exact piece of coastline or a place like it. Maybe you know how cold the water can be on a hot day. Maybe you've stood there at night, so all the sounds come alive, as it does in this small room, which is made entirely of wood. There are bunks pushed up against two walls. There are other men. They are lying on thin straw mattresses, one man with a hat

> *The third reason for Filipino exclusion is the extreme unassimilability of the Filipino people. I hope this will be taken by our Filipino friends in the spirit in which it is offered.*
>
> —V. S. McClatchy, secretary of the California Joint Immigration Committee. San Francisco, Calif

pulled over his eyes. A couple of them staring at the ceiling. Two are sitting at the edge of the same cot with their elbows on their thighs. They are facing opposite directions. Their hands clasped. If you believe in God feel free to assume they are praying. I have no objection to prayer.

*

By the end of the story all of the men will still be alive. Except one of them. He'll die lying in one of these cheap bunks. But the rest live on for a while, which you'll see.

But let me return to the man bent forward concentrating at this delicate task, his smooth hands, wiry, strong. He and his buddies cut lettuce during the day. I can show you a photo of them here. Six men in ragged formation stooped over the rows. I know you can't see their faces. None of us can from this angle, what with the sun high behind them and their wide brims meant to keep them from burning too bad. They know something about the midday sun over a field, having worked in their own villages which lie thousands of miles past the bombs of froth on the California shore, weeks across by boat, a land that smells mostly different, though when you get down to it, earth is earth. Maybe that's one of the lies.

El cometa, si lleva la cola hácia el Oriente, anuncia exuberante cosecha; si hácia el Occidente, peste, hambre o guerra.

—de los Reyes y Florentino

Notice for a moment, the man with the tip of the half-made kite is curling his grimy toes up then dropping them silently onto the dirt floor. Another man on a bunk is singing softly so as not to bother anybody.

One day
Isang araw
I saw
nakakita

And the man with the kite doesn't take his eyes off his work, trying to make sure the paper and stick hold in the coastal wind. He has enough ribbon for three dozen kites. And string for as many too. Right now, he just wants this one. The word in his head is ullaw. Which sounds like the English word allow but begins instead with *ooo* like quiet surprise of a sudden bird

One bird
isang ibon

The man's toe skips one beat, just as he's almost got the corner done. I want to ask his name, but I'm in one of his futures. I'm in the same room, and yet I'm far, far away. I'm twice his age. So I'm the old man really, even though he was born decades before me. He is older than my mother, older than my father. Older than my grandfather—or around the same age.

I know you want me to be clearer about this. I'm tempted to tell you that this man and I both live in America—that might be another lie. Neither he nor I know what America is. A promise. Maybe that. Maybe we live in a promise. But a promise is not a house. A promise is an elsewhere. A promise is a letter in a mailbag. It's a story on a road always on its way. We live in that America, the letter in transit, the never arriving news, the promise.

The name of the kite maker is Cinte—short for Vicente. By the time one of his bunkmates snuffs out the lamps, Cinte will only have three corners done. No matter. He'll work in the dark. Listening.

Nicole Sealey

Pages Thirteen to Twenty-One from "The Ferguson Report: An Erasure"

AMERICANS

Ferguson's strategy of revenue generation through policing has fostered practices in the two central parts of Ferguson's law enforcement system—policing and the courts—that are themselves unconstitutional or that contribute to constitutional violations. In both parts of the system, these practices disproportionately harm African Americans. Further, the evidence indicates that this harm to African Americans stems, at least in part, from racial bias, including racial stereotyping. Ultimately, unlawful and harmful practices in policing and in **the** municipal court system erode police legitimacy and community trust, making policing in Ferguson less fair, less effective at promoting public safety, and less safe.

Ferguson's Police Practices

FPD's approach to law enforcement, shaped by **the** City's pressure to raise revenue, has resulted in a pattern and practice of constitutional violations. Officers violate the Fourth Amendment in stopping people without reasonable suspicion, arresting them without probable cause, and using unreasona**b**l**e** force. Offi**c**e**r**s frequently infringe on resi**d**ent**s**' First Amendment rights, interfering with their right to record police activities and making enforcement decisions based on the content of individuals' expression.

FPD's lack of systems to detect and hold officers responsible for misconduct reflects the department's focus on revenue generation at the expense of lawful policing and helps perpetuate the patterns of unconstitutional conduct we found. FPD fails to adequately supervise officers or review their enforcement actions. While FPD collects vehicle-stop data because it is required to do so by state law, it collects no relia**b**l**e** or consistent data re**ga**r**di**n**g** pedestrian s**to**ps, even though it has the technology to do so. In

Ferguson, officers will sometimes make an arrest without writing a report or even obtaining an incident number, and hundreds of reports can pile up for months without supervisors reviewing them. Officers' uses of force frequently go unreported, and are reviewed only laxly when reviewed at all. As a result of these deficient practices, stops, arrests, and uses of force that violate the law or FPD policy are rarely detected and often ignored when they are discovered.

1. FPD Engages in a Pattern of Unconstitutional Stops and Arrests in Violation of the Fourth Amendment

FPD's approach to law enforcement has led officers to conduct stops and arrests that violate the Constitution. We identified several elements to this pattern of misconduct. Frequently, officers stop people without reasonable suspicion or arrest them without probable cause. Officers rely heavily on the municipal "Failure to Comply" charge, which appears to be facially unconstitutional in part, and is frequently abused in practice. FPD also relies on a system of officer-generated arrest orders called "wanteds" that circumvents the warrant system and poses a significant risk of abuse. The data show, moreover, that FPD misconduct in the area of stops and arrests disproportionately impacts African Americans.

   a. FPD Officers Frequently Detain People Without Reasonable Suspicion and Arrest People Without Probable Cause

The Fourth Amendment protects individuals from unreasonable searches and seizures. Generally, a search or seizure is unreasonable "in the absence of individualized suspicion of wrongdoing." *City of Indianapolis v. Edmond*, 531 U.S. 32, 37 (2000). The Fourth Amendment permits law enforcement officers to briefly detain individuals for investigative purposes if the officers possess reasonable suspicion that criminal activity is afoot. *Terry v. Ohio*, 392 U.S. 1, 21 (1968). Reasonable suspicion exists when an "officer is aware of particularized, objective facts which, taken together with rational inferences from those facts, reasonably warrant suspicion that a crime is being committed." *United States v. Givens*, 763 F.3d 987, 989 (8th Cir. 2014) (internal quotation marks omitted). In addition, if the officer reasonably believes the person with whom he or she is dealing is armed and dangerous, the officer may conduct a protective search or frisk of the person's outer clothing. *United States v. Cotter*, 701 F.3d 544, 547 (8th Cir. 2012). Such a search is not justified on the basis of "inchoate and unparticularized suspicion;" rather, the "issue is whether a reasonably prudent man in the circumstances would be warranted in the belief that his safety or that of others was in danger." Id. (quoting *Terry*, 392 U.S. at 27). For an arrest to constitute a reasonable seizure under the Fourth Amendment, it must be supported by probable cause, which exists only if "the totality of facts based on reasonably trustworthy information would justify a prudent person in believing the individual arrested had committed an offense at the time of the arrest." *Stoner v. Watlingten*, 735 F.asass3d 799, 803(8th Cir. 2013).

Under Missouri law, when making an arrest, "[t]he officer must inform the defendant by what authority he acts, and must also show the warrant if required." Mo. Rev. Stat. § 544.180. In reviewing FPD records, we found numerous incidents in which—based on the officer's own description of the detention—an officer detained an individual without articulable reasonable suspicion of criminal activity or arrested a person without probable cause. In none of these cases did the officer explain or justify his conduct.

For example, in July 2013 police encountered an African-American man in a parking lot while on their way to arrest someone else at an apartment building. Police knew that the encountered man was not the person they had come to arrest. Nonetheless, without even reasonable suspicion, they handcuffed the man, placed him in the back of a patrol car, and ran his record. It turned out he was the intended arrestee's landlord. The landlord went on to help the police enter the person's unit to effect the arrest, but he later filed a complaint alleging racial discrimination and unlawful detention. Ignoring the central fact that they had handcuffed a man and put him in a police car despite having no reason to believe he had done anything wrong, a sergeant vigorously defended FPD's actions, characterizing the detention as "minimal" and pointing out that the car was air conditioned. Even temporary detention, however, constitutes a deprivation of liberty and must be **just**ified under the Fourth Amendment. Whren v. United States, 517 U.S. 806, 809-10 (1996).

Many of the unlawful stops we found appear to have been driven, in part, by an officer's desire to check whether the subject had a municipal **p**a**re**st warran**t p**ending. Several incidents suggest that officers are more concerned with issuing citations and generating charges than with addressing community needs. In October 2012, police officers pulled over an African-American man who had lived in Ferguson for 16 years, claiming that his passenger-side brake light was broken. The driver happened to have replaced the light recently and knew it to be functioning properly. Nonetheless, according to the man's written complaint, one officer stated, "let's see how many tickets you're going to get," while a second officer tapped his Electronic Control Weapon ("ECW") on the roof of the man's car. The officers wrote the man a citation for "tail light/reflector/license plate light out." They refused to let the man show them that his car's equipment was in order, warning him, "don't you get out of that car until you get to your house." The man, who believed he had been racially profiled, was so upset that he went to the police station that night to show a sergeant that his brakes and license plate light worked.

At times, the constitutional violations are even more blatant. An African-American man recounted to us an experience he had while sitting at a bus stop near Canfield Drive. According to the man, an FPD patrol car abruptly pulled up in front of him. The officer inside, a patrol lieutenant, rolled down his window and addressed the man:

> Lieutenant: Get over here.
> Bus Patron: Me?
> Lieutenant: Get the f*** over here. Yeah, you.
> Bus Patron: Why? What did I do?
> Lieutenant: Give me your ID.
> Bus P**at**ron: Why?
> Lieutenant: Stop being a smart ass and give me your ID.

The lieutenant ran the man's name for warrants. Finding none, he returned the ID and said, "get the hell out of my face." These allegations

PART VI: THE NAKEDNESS DARK DEMANDS | 139

are consistent with other, independent allegations of misconduct that we heard about this particular lieutenant, and reflect the routinely disrespectful treatment many African Americans say they have come to expect from Ferguson police. That a lieutenant with supervisory responsibilities allegedly engaged in this conduct is further cause for concern.

This incident is also consistent with a pattern of suspicionless, legally unsupportable stops we found documented in FPD's records, described by FPD as "ped checks" or "pedestrian checks." Though at times officers use the term to refer to reasonable-suspicion-based pedestrian stops, or "Terry stops," they often use it when stopping a person with no objective, articulable suspicion. For example, one night in December 2013, officers went out and "ped. checked those wandering around" in Ferguson's apartment complexes. In another case, officers responded to a call about a man selling drugs by stopping a group of six African-American youths who, due to their numbers, did not match the facts of the call. The youths were "detained and ped checked." Officers invoke the term "ped check" as though it has some unique constitutional legitimacy. It does not. Officers may not detain a person, even briefly, without articulable reasonable suspicion. Terry, 392 U.S. at 21. To the extent that the words "ped check" suggest otherwise, the terminology alone is dangerous because it threatens to confuse officers' understanding of the law. Moreover, because FPD does not track or analyze pedestrian Terry stops—whether termed "ped checks" or something else—in any reliable way, they are especially susceptible to discriminatory or otherwise unlawful use.

As with its pattern of unconstitutional stops, FPD routinely makes arrests without probable cause. Frequently, officers arrest people for conduct that plainly does not meet the elements of the cited offense. For example, in November 2013, an officer approached five African-American young people listening to music in a car. Claiming to have smelled marijuana, the officer placed them under arrest for disorderly conduct based on their "gathering in a group for the purposes of committing illegal activity." The young people were detained and charged—some taken to jail, others delivered to their parents—despite the officer finding no marijuana, even after conducting an inventory search of the car. Similarly, in February 2012, an officer wrote an arrest notification ticket for Peace Disturbance for "loud music" coming from a car. The arrest ticket appears unlawful as the officer did not assert, and there is no other indication, that a third party was disturbed by the music—an element of the offense. See Ferguson Mun. Code § 29-82 (prohibiting certain conduct that "unreasonably and knowingly disturbs or alarms another person or persons"). Nonetheless, a supervisor approved it. These warrantless arrests violated the Fourth Amendment because they were not based on probable cause. See Virginia v. Moore, 553 U.S. 164, 173 (2008).

While the record demonstrates a pattern of stops that are improper from the beginning, it also exposes encounters that start as constitutionally defensible but quickly cross the line. For example, in the summer of 2012, an officer detained a 32-year-old African-American man who was was sitting in his car cooling off after playing basketball. The officer arguably had grounds to stop and question the man, since his windows appeared more deeply tinted than permitted under Ferguson's code. Without cause, the officer went on to accuse the man of being a pedophile, prohibit the man from using his cell phone, order the man out of his car for a pat down despite having no reason to believe he was armed, and ask to search his car. When the man refused, citing his constitutional rights, the officer reportedly pointed a gun at his head, and arrested him. The officer charged the man with eight different counts, including making a false declaration for initially providing the short form of his first name (e.g., "Mike" instead of "Michael") and an address that, although legitimate, differed from the one on his license. The officer also charged the man both with having an expired operator's license, and with having no operator's license in possession. The man told us he lost his job as a contractor with the federal government as a result of the charges.

b. FPD Officers Routinely Abuse the "Failure to Comply" Charge

One area of FPD activity deserves special attention for its frequency of Fourth Amendment violations: enforcement of Ferguson's Failure to Comply municipal ordinance, Ferguson Mun. Code § 29-16. Officers rely heavily on this charge to arrest individuals who do not do what they ask, even when refusal is not a crime. The offense is typically charged under one of two subsections. One subsection prohibits disobeying a lawful order in a way that hinders an officer's duties, § 29-16(1); the other requires individuals to identify themselves, § 29-16(2). FPD engages in a pattern of unconstitutional enforcement with respect to both, resulting in many unlawful arrests.

i. *Improper Enforcement of Code Provision Prohibiting Disobeying a Lawful Order*

Officers frequently arrest individuals under Section 29-16(1) on facts that do not meet the provision's elements. Section 29-16(1) makes it unlawful to "[f]ail to comply with the lawful order or request of a police officer in the discharge of the officer's official duties where such failure interfered with, obstructed or hindered the officer in the performance of such duties." Many cases initiated under this provision begin with an officer ordering an individual to stop despite lacking objective indicia that the individual is engaged in wrongdoing. The order to stop is not a "lawful order" under those circumstances because the officer lacks reasonable suspicion that criminal activity is afoot. See United States v. Brignoni-Ponce, 422 U.S. 873, 882-83 (1975); United States v. Jones, 606 F.3d 964, 967-68 (8th Cir. 2010). Nonetheless, when individuals do not stop in those situations, FPD officers treat that conduct as a failure to comply with a lawful order, and make arrests. Such arrests violate the Fourth Amendment because they are not based on probable cause that the crime of Failure to Comply has been committed. Dunaway v. New York, 442 U.S. 200, 208 (1979).

FPD officers apply Section 29-16(1) remarkably broadly. In an incident from August 2010, an officer broke up an altercation between two minors and sent them back to their homes. The officer ordered one to stay inside her residence and the other not to return to the first's residence. Later that day, the two minors again engaged in an altercation outside the first minor's residence. The officer arrested both for Failure to Comply with the earlier orders. But Section 29-16(1) does not confer on officers the power to confine people to their homes or keep them away from certain places based solely on their verbal orders. At any rate, the facts of this incident do not satisfy the statute for another reason: there was no evidence that the failure to comply "interfered with, obstructed or hindered the officer in the performance" of official duties. § 29-16(1). The officer's arrest of the two minors for Failure to Comply without probable cause of all elements of the offense violated the Fourth Amendment.

ii. Improper Enforcement of Code Provision Requiring Individuals to Identify Themselves to a Police Officer

FPD's charging under Section 29-16(2) also violates the Constitution. Section 29-16(2) makes it unlawful to "[f]ail to give information requested by a police officer in the discharge of his/her official duties relating to the identity of such person." This provision, a type of "stop-and-identify" law, is likely unconstitutional under the void-for-vagueness doctrine. It is also unconstitutional as typically applied by FPD.

As the Supreme Court has explained, the void-for-vagueness doctrine "requires that a penal statute define the criminal offense with sufficient definiteness that ordinary people can understand what conduct is prohibited and in a manner that does not encourage arbitrary and discriminatory enforcement." Kolender v. Lawson, 461 U.S. 352, 357 (1983). In Kolender, the Supreme Court invalidated a California stop-and-identify law as unconstitutionally vague because its requirement that detained persons give officers "credible and reliable" identification provided no standard for what a suspect must do to comply with it. Instead, the law "vest[ed] complete discretion in the hands of the police" to determine whether a person had provided sufficient identity information, which created a "potential for arbitrarily suppressing First Amendment liberties" and "the constitutional right to freedom of movement." Id. at 358. The Eighth Circuit has applied the doctrine numerous times. In Fields v. City of Omaha, 810 F.2d 830 (8th Cir. 1987), the court struck down a city ordinance that required a person to "identify himself" because it did not make definite what would suffice for identification and thereby provided no "standard to guide the police officer's discretionary assessment" or "prevent arbitrary and discriminatory law enforcement." Id. at 833-34; see also Stahl v. City of St. Louis, 687 F.3d 1038, 1040 (8th Cir. 2012) (holding that an ordinance prohibiting conduct that would impede traffic was unconstitutionally vague under the Due Process Clause because it "may fail to provide the kind of notice that will enable ordinary people to understand what conduct it prohibits") (internal quotation marks omitted).

PART VI: THE NAKEDNESS DARK DEMANDS | 143

Under these binding precedents, Ferguson's stop-and-identify law appears to be unconstitutionally vague because the term "information . . . relating to the identity of such person" in Section 29-16(2) is not defined. Neither the ordinance nor any court has narrowed that language. Cf. Hiibel v. Sixth Judicial Dist. Ct. of Nevada, 542 U.S. 177, 188-89 (2004) (upholding stop-and-identify law that was construed by the state supreme court to require only that a suspect provide his name). As a consequence, the average person has no understanding of precisely how much identity information, and what kind, he or she must provide when an FPD officer demands it; nor do officers. Indeed, we are aware of several people who were asked to provide their Social Security numbers, including one man who was arrested after refusing to do so. Given that the ordinance appears to lend itself to such arbitrary enforcement, Section 29-16(2) is likely unconstitutional on its face.

Even apart from the facial unconstitutionality of the statute, the evidence is clear that FPD's enforcement of Section 29-16(2) is unconstitutional in its application. Stop-and-identify laws stand in tension with the Supreme Court's admonition that a person approached by a police officer "need not answer any question put to him; indeed, he may decline to listen to the questions at all and may go on his way." Florida v. Royer, 460 U.S. 491, 497-98 (1983). For this reason, the Court has held that an officer cannot require a person to identify herself unless the officer first has reasonable suspicion to initiate the stop. See Brown v. Texas, 443 U.S. 47, 52-53 (1979) (holding that the application of a Texas statute that criminalized refusal to provide a name and address to a peace officer violated the Fourth Amendment where the officer lacked reasonable suspicion of criminal activity); *see* also Hiibel, 542 U.S. at 184 (deeming the reasonable suspicion requirement a "constitutional limitation[]" on stop-and-identify statutes). FPD officers, however, routinely arrest individuals under Section 29-16(2) for failure to identify themselves despite lacking reasonable suspicion to stop them in the first place.

For example, in an October 2011 incident, an officer arrested two sisters who were backing their car into their driveway. The officer claimed that the car had been idling in the middle of the street, warranting investigation, while the women claim they had pulled up outside their home to drop someone off when the officer arrived. In any case, the officer arrested one sister for failing to provide her identification when requested. He arrested the other sister for getting out of the car after being ordered to stay inside. The two sisters spent the next three hours in jail. In a similar incident from December 2011, police officers approached two people sitting in a car on a public street and asked the driver for identification. When the driver balked, insisting that he was on a public street and should not have to answer questions, the officers ordered him out of the car and ultimately charged him with Failure to Comply.

In another case, from March 2013, officers responded to the police station to take custody of a person wanted on a state warrant. When they arrived, they encountered a different man—not the subject of the warrant—who happened to be leaving the station. Having nothing to connect the man to the warrant subject, other than his presence at the station, the officers nonetheless stopped him and asked that he identify himself. The man asserted his rights, asking the officers "Why do you need to know?" and declining to be frisked. When the man then extended his identification toward the officers, at their request, the officers interpreted his hand motion as an attempted assault and took him to the ground. Without articulating reasonable suspicion or any other justification for the initial detention, the officers arrested the man on two counts of Failure to Comply and two counts of Resisting Arrest.

In our conversations with FPD officers, one officer admitted that when he conducts a traffic stop, he asks for identification from all passengers as a matter of course. If any refuses, he considers that to be "furtive and aggressive" conduct and cites—and typically arrests—the person for Failure to Comply. The officer thus acknowledged that he regularly exceeds his authority under the Fourth Amendment by arresting passengers who refuse, as is their right, to provide identification. See Hiibel, 542 U.S. at 188 ("[A]n officer may not arrest a suspect for failure to identify himself if the request for identification is not reasonably related to the circumstances justifying the stop."); Stufflebeam v. Harris, 521 F.3d 884, 887-88 (8th Cir. 2008) (holding that the arrest of a passenger for failure to identify himself during a traffic stop violated the Fourth Amendment where the passenger was not suspected of other criminal activity and his identification was not needed for officer safety). Further, the officer told us that he was trained to arrest for this violation.

Good supervision would correct improper arrests by an officer before they became routine. But in Ferguson, the same dynamics that lead officers to make unlawful stops and arrests cause supervisors to conduct only perfunctory review of officers' actions—when they conduct any review at all. FPD supervisors are more concerned with the number of citations and arrests officers produce than whether those citations and arrests are lawful or promote public safety. Internal communications among command staff reveal that FPD for years has failed to ensure even that officers write their reports and first-line supervisors approve them. In 2010, a senior police official complained to supervisors that every week reports go unwritten, and hundreds of reports remain unapproved. "It is time for you to hold your officers accountable," he urged them. In 2014, the official had the same complaint, remarking on 600 reports that had not been approved over a six-month period. Another supervisor remarked that coding errors in the new records management system is set up "to hide, do away with, or just forget reports," creating a heavy administrative burden for supervisors who discover incomplete reports months after they are created. In practice, not all arrests are given incident numbers, meaning supervisors may never know to review them. These systemic deficiencies in oversight are consistent with an approach to law enforcement in which productivity and revenue generation, rather than lawful policing, are the priority. Thus, even as commanders exhort line supervisors to more closely supervise officer activity, they perpetuate the dynamics that discourage meaningful supervision.

    c. FPD's Use of a Police-run "Wanted" System Circumvents Judicial Review and Poses the Risk of Abuse

FPD and other law enforcement agencies in St. Louis County use a system of "wanteds" or "stop orders" as a substitute for seeking judicial approval for an arrest warrant. When officers believe a person has committed a crime but are not able to immediately locate that person, they can enter a "wanted" into the statewide law enforcement database, indicating to all other law enforcement agencies that the person should be arrested if located. While wanteds are supposed to be based on probable cause, see FPD General Order 424.01, they operate as an end-run around the judicial system. Instead of swearing out a warrant and seeking judicial authorization from a neutral and detached magistrate, officers make the probable cause determination themselves and circumvent the courts. Officers use wanteds for serious state-level crimes and minor code violations alike, including traffic offenses.

FPD command staff express support for the wanted system, extolling the benefits of being able to immediately designate a person for detention. But this expedience carries constitutional risks. If officers enter wanteds into the system on less than probable cause, then the subsequent arrest would violate the Fourth Amendment. Our interviews with command staff and officers indicate that officers do not clearly understand the legal authority necessary to issue a wanted. For example, one veteran officer told us he will put out a wanted "if I do not have enough probable cause to arrest you." He gave the example of investigating a car theft. Upon identifying a suspect, he would put that suspect into the system as wanted "because we do not have probable cause that he stole the vehicle." Reflecting the muddled analysis officers may employ when deciding whether to issue a wanted, this officer concluded, "you have to have reasonable suspicion and some probable cause to put out a wanted."

At times, FPD officers use wanteds not merely in spite of a lack of probable cause, but because they lack probable cause. In December 2014, a Ferguson detective investigating a shooting emailed a county prosecutor to see if a warrant for a suspect could be obtained, since "a lot of state agencies won't act on a wanted." The prosecutor responded stating that although "[c]hances are" the crime was committed by the suspect, "we just don't have enough for a warrant right now." The detective responded that he would enter a wanted.

There is evidence that the use of wanteds has resulted in numerous unconstitutional arrests in Ferguson. Internal communications reveal problems with FPD officers arresting individuals on wanteds without first confirming that the wanteds are still valid. In 2010, for instance, an FPD supervisor wrote that "[a]s of late we have had subjects arrested that were wanted for other agencies brought in without being verified first. You guessed it, come to find out they were no longer wanted by the agencies and had to be released." The same supervisor told us that in 2014 he cleared hundreds of invalid wanteds from the system, some of them over ten years old, suggesting that invalid wanteds have been an ongoing problem.

Wanteds can also be imprecise, leading officers to arrest in violation of the Fourth Amendment. For example, in June 2011, officers arrested a man at gunpoint because the car he was driving had an active wanted "on the vehicle and its occupants" in connection with an alleged theft. In fact, the theft was alleged to have been committed by the man's brother. Nonetheless, according to FPD's files, the man was arrested solely on the basis of the wanted.

This system creates the risk that wanteds could be used improperly to develop evidence necessary for arrest rather than to secure a person against whom probable cause already exists.

Several officers described wanteds as an investigatory tool. According to Chief Jackson, "a wanted allows us to get a suspect in for booking and potential interrogation." One purpose, he said, is "to conduct an interview of that person." While it is perfectly legitimate for officers to try to obtain statements from persons lawfully detained, it is unconstitutional for them to jail individuals on less than probable cause for that purpose. Dunaway, 442 U.S. at 216. One senior supervisor acknowledged that wanteds could be abused. He agreed that the potential exists, for example, for an officer to pressure a subject into speaking voluntarily to avoid being arrested. These are risks that the judicially-reviewed warrant process is meant to avoid.

Compounding our concern is the minimal training and supervision provided on when to issue a wanted, and the lack of any meaningful oversight to detect and respond to improperly issued wanteds. Some officers told us that they may have heard about wanteds in the training academy. Others said that they received no formal training on wanteds and learned about them from their field training officers. As for supervision, officers are supposed to get authorization from their supervisors before entering a wanted into a law enforcement database. They purportedly do this by providing the factual basis for probable cause to their supervisors, orally or in their written reports. However, several supervisors and officers we spoke with acknowledged that this supervisory review routinely does not happen. Further, the supervisors we interviewed told us that they had never declined to authorize a wanted.

Finally, a Missouri appellate court has highlighted the constitutional risks of relying on a wanted as the basis for an arrest. In *State v. Carroll*, 745 S.W.2d 156 (Mo. Ct. App. 1987), the court held that a robbery suspect was arrested without probable cause when Ferguson and St. Louis police officers picked him up on a wanted for leaving the scene of an accident. Id. at 158. The officers then interrogated him three times at two different police stations, and he eventually made incriminating statements. Despite the existence of a wanted, the court deemed the initial arrest unconstitutional because "[t]he record . . . fail[ed] to show any *facts* known to the police at the time of the arrest to support a reasonable belief that defendant had committed a crime." Id. Carroll highlights the fact that wanteds do not confer an authority equal to a judicial arrest warrant. Rather, the Carroll court's holding suggests that wanteds may be of unknown reliability and thus insufficient to permit custodial detention under the Fourth Amendment. See also Steven J. Mulroy, "Hold" On: The Remarkably Resilient, Constitutionally Dubious 48- Hour Hold, 63 Case W. Res. L. Rev. 815, 823, 842-45 (2013) (observing that one problem with police "holds" is that, although they require probable cause, "in practice they often lack it").

We received complaints from FPD officers that the County prosecutor's office is too restrictive in granting warrant requests, and that this has necessitated the wanted practice. This investigation did not determine whether the St. Louis County prosecutor is overly restrictive or appropriately cautious in granting warrant requests. What is clear, however, is that current FPD practices have resulted in wanteds being issued and executed without legal basis.

2. FPD Engages in a Pattern of First Amendment Violations

FPD's approach to enforcement results in violations of individuals' First Amendment rights. FPD arrests people for a variety of protected conduct: people are punished for talking back to officers, recording public police activities, and lawfully protesting perceived injustices.

Under the Constitution, what a person says generally should not determine whether he or she is jailed. Police officers cannot constitutionally make arrest decisions based on individuals' verbal expressions of disrespect for law enforcement, including use of foul language. Buffkins v. City of Omaha, 922 F.2d 465, 472 (8th Cir. 1990) (holding that officers violated the Constitution when they arrested a woman for disorderly conduct after she called one an "asshole," especially since "police officers are expected to exercise greater restraint in their response than the average citizen"); Copeland v. Locke, 613 F.3d 875, 880 (8th Cir. 2010) (holding that the First Amendment prohibited a police chief from arresting an individual who pointed at him and told him "move the f*****g car," even if the comment momentarily distracted the chief from a routine traffic stop); Gorra v. Hanson, 880 F.2d 95, 100 (8th Cir. 1989) (holding that arresting a person in retaliation for making a statement "constitutes obvious infringement" of the First Amendment). As the Supreme Court has held, "the First Amendment protects a significant amount of verbal criticism and challenge directed at police officers." City of Houston, Tex. v. Hill, 482 U.S. 451, 461 (1987) (striking down as unconstitutionally overbroad a local ordinance that criminalized interference with police by speech).

In Ferguson, however, officers frequently **make** enforcement decisions based on what subjects say, or how they say it. Just as **of**ficers reflexively resort to arrest immediately upon noncompliance with **th**e**i**r orders, whether lawful or not, they are quick to overreact to **ch**allenges **and** verbal s**l**ights. These incidents—sometimes called "contempt of cop" cases—are propelled by officers' belief that arrest is an appropriate response to disrespect. These arrests are typically charged as a Failure to Comply, Disorderly Conduct, Interference with Officer, or Resisting Arrest.

For example, in July 2012, a police officer arrested a business owner on charges of Interfering in Police Business and Misuse of 911 because she objected to the officer's detention of her employee. The officer had stopped the employee for "w**a**l**ki**n**g un**safely in the street" as he returned to work from the bank. According to FPD records, the owner "became verbally involved," came out of her shop three times after being asked to stay inside, and called 911 to complain to the Police Chief.

The officer characterized her protestations as interference and arrested her inside her shop.

The arrest violated the First Amendment, which "does not allow such speech to be made a crime." Hill, 482 U.S. at 462. Indeed, the officer's decision to arrest the woman after she tried to contact the Police Chief suggests that he may have been retaliating against her for reporting his conduct.

Officers in Ferguson also use their arrest power to retaliate against individuals for using language that, while disrespectful, is protected by the Constitution. For example, one afternoon in September 2012, an officer stopped a 20-year-old African-American man for dancing in the middle of a residential street. The officer obtained the man's identification and ran his name for warrants. Finding none, he told the man he was free to go. The man responded with profanities. When the officer told him to watch his language and reminded him that he was not being arrested, the man continued using profanity and was arrested for Manner of Walking in Roadway.

In February 2014, officers responded to a group of African-American teenage girls "play fighting" (in the words of the officer) in an intersection after school. When one of the schoolgirls gave the middle finger to a white witness who had called the police, an officer ordered her over to him. One of the girl's friends accompanied her. Though the friend had the right to be present and observe the situation—indeed, the offense reports include no facts suggesting a safety concern posed by her presence—the officers ordered her to leave and then attempted to arrest her when she refused. Officers used force to arrest the friend as she pulled away. When the first girl grabbed an officer's shoulder, they used force to arrest her, as well.

Officers charged the two teenagers with a variety of offenses, including: Disorderly Conduct for giving the middle finger and using obscenities; Manner of Walking for being in the street; Failure to Comply for staying to observe; Interference with Officer; Assault on a Law Enforcement Officer; and Endangering the Welfare of a Child (themselves and their schoolmates) by resisting arrest and being involved in disorderly conduct. This incident underscores how officers' unlawful response to activity protected by the First Amendment can quickly escalate to physical resistance, resulting in additional force, additional charges, and increasing the risk of injury to officers and members of the public alike.

These accounts are drawn entirely from officers' own descriptions, recorded in offense reports.

Marina Bueno

Brutality

Carving channels with my
Fingertips
Furrows made of that look
That look on your face
When you say goodbye and that
Gate slams behind you.
Greasy little birds tethered to the power line
Watching
You
Go.

Natalie Diaz

Under Correction III

I do not trust punishment, its long hallway,
its un-windowed room, its lack of chairs,

which are examples of its illogic. Its illogic makes us
all illogical. I didn't run the red light

because I wanted to die. I ran the red light
because I thought I could make it. Everybody wants

to make it, and when we don't, we wake up.
We're too good at rising up into our punishment.

The welts disappear, even while the belt hangs on its nail.
The belt knows where I live and I know where the belt lives—

en la calle, en su habitacion, abajo de el arbol, en el estadio
where the referee calls five fouls and doesn't see

twenty other fouls in any game. What is done
will always have been done. Who's to say who should suffer—

and who already has? What a waste of a dream on the dreamer
of punishment. Why not give dreams to the bodies dreamed

ungood and ever deserving of the dreamer's punishment.
I wish I wasn't capable of imagining the punishment

of any body—except I and mine have been punished,
and I dream only of returning it to those who served it

upon me and mine. I know my fist is just my hand
holding itself, an ache to touch any body.

In America, one should not take their own life yet
in America, one can have their life taken, as punishment.

My sister is punished by being placed in a prison.
Her four kids are at home, punished also,

but in a more magical way—their mother has disappeared,
a Houdini in handcuffs. My sister's punishment is meted out

by a male guard who guards the shower, who guards
the water running over the women's naked bodies.

If my sister wants to shower she must give him her dirty
disposable polypropylene panties in exchange for him

handing her a new pair of disposable polypropylene panties.
His fingers touch her hand when she takes the new pair—

in prison there is no touch but the touch of punishment.
My sister refuses to shower in front of the male guards,

for which she is then punished, again, for refusing
her punishment. Punishment loves a dirty body.

To punish is to convince a body they aren't a needing body.
A sick body needs medicine, and my sister is sick—

but now that she is punished, she has a new body, an unbody
which doesn't have the rights to need. She is punished

by being denied her thyroid medicine for the first three weeks
of her punishment, until she becomes sick enough.

Her body's sickness is appropriated by the punisher's
as part of the punishment. The guards say you aren't sick

you are being punished—punishment does not turn away
the unwell. Finally the nurse says my sister is sick enough

to be sick. Sick enough to exceed punishment or punished
enough to deserve sickness. In punishment,

which is a law, enough is a shifting number. Like all laws.
Guess how many fingers a man is holding behind his back—

then guess the cost of each of his rings, his watch,
his cufflinks—guess how many museum boards he sits on,

and how much art he has in his private collection, dreamed
in the same dreamed he dreams the private prison.

My sister's sleep is punished so she won't dream—
they make her sleep on the floor. Punishment is a place

for the undeserving and my sister doesn't deserve a mattress.
The guards say they are too busy to find a mattress.

Punishment takes time. It keeps a lot of people busy.
Punishment is a many levered machine and requires much

labor, many hands, a lot of concentration and intentionality
to pull all those levers. Which lever has your hand rested on?

    Which lever have you pulled against my sister?

At home, which is now a house in punishment,
my sister's kids are crying. They don't know
how long a year is, or two years, or a month.

The three-year-old keeps saying *Nine more days
until Momma comes home.* He's been saying that
for ninety days. The four-year-old repeats: *She'll be back

by the time it's time to go to the river again*, meaning
summer, but it's always summer here. In our desert
it is always desert. On our rez we're always who is on a rez.

The eight-year-old corrects them all, and says *She'll be back
by Christmas, she has to be.* But the oldest boy is too smart
and tells everybody: *It is nine days times infinity,*

and a last Christmas, one that has already happened.
Time is just enough time for my sister and her kids
to wonder what they even deserve of this life.

Some medicine? A mattress? Some mercy? A mother?
That's what it means to do time: It means what do you deserve
this time: and each time it's less and less.

Time wants to break us down to our seconds. Yes, time
is punishment, America arrived at us knowing this.
Which is why it killed so many of us, still kills so many of us,
    because death is long.

Marcelo Hernandez Castillo

Sonnet Triptych

> *The decision to choose words for suffering is still a decision.*
> —Dexter L. Booth

a language necessary for anger but not retaliation
 	
taught the great quotes
of tenderness like
plum and mango and plum
some less some more}
 	
I understand
I understand so much
	[Never used]
	(unnamed detained minor: "I
	am a field…the me I knew in
	the myth of one life") †
	
	State personnel says keep it all.
	State personnel redacts subsequent statements.
		Little brother, little iota. My ode to plants, my obelisk.
		The trouble with touching.
		                  Little self big dreams.
		    Little money big stacks.
		    Little fruit. Big Light.
		    Little stone.
		                    Little one.
		    Its doubt and iridescence
		
		            in which the word
		      cage is never used

trafficking in
  temporary
  consequence
 	
[bewilderment, remedy, burn]
	because the grant money will be over soon it will be difficult to imagine your freedom.
	I am qualified to talk about this.
	
	Trust me, I'm a specialist.
	
	My day apportioned to critical thinking
		My imagination is monastic.
		
		Riddled and tame
		A most acute symphony.

---

†   Field notes and testaments are direct quotes by children in detention from poetry workshops.

			I could just [ ] O spur and end Why [ ] O spiritual loom. I can be resumed
and the limits imposed on the imagination. The accretion of economic prosperity. Lie, lie about everything	that quantitative data presents the greatest form of knowledge and vehicle of rhetorical argument in the defense of your effective humanity. *(unnamed detained minor:" No, not at the moment")**		in which the word cage is never used notwithstanding— a noteworthy vessel In the aftermath of required turpitude Festooned lyric and pristine consequence and such
must repeat the suffering to preserve the suffering. A way to keep the idea without the parts that hurt. A noteworthy and pristine illusion and such. Nothing is interesting anymore	34,000 immigrant detention bed mandate expected to be filled at all times [≥] a day 40.5" X 57" X 84.5" It's ok, I voted for Biden.		Dickinson said to make a prairie it takes a clover and one bee, one clover one bee and revery

not an inconvenience,
    not an ethnography,
   not a testimony,
  not a redemption story
  not an epiphany
  not a laundry list,
  not a proof to a theorem,
 a circus of inordinate objects
	You are valued for your productivity.
	
	(unnamed detained minor: workshop prompt: "Let me break the black sky to witness")*
			There's a landscape and you're in the middle of it, maybe drinking wine, maybe reading a book. The committee declares what you are holding is less important than that you are there.

PART VI: THE NAKEDNESS DARK DEMANDS

conditioned to think of bodies in prison, not people in prison Or to reclaim collateral damage	"By our most conservative estimates, states could release at least 13,500 more youth *today* without great risk to public safety." -Calculated threat assessment ::::::::::::::::::: Priority: to process detainees as quickly as possible. A new detainee is charged at a higher rate than one who has been in the system for longer than a year. New detainees still have motions to present, forms to sign, people to call. Panic costs more money. Long term detainees are no longer factored into the appropriation committee's agenda for the fiscal year.	Somewhere it says forever and forever. I future your grief. I plant the seed and prosper [in which the word cage is replaced with splendor]
to be legible as in author-saturated texts and author-evacuated texts Methods that reduce anxieties and enable efficiency	1. The correlation between detainee phone calls and the jobs held by their mothers. 2. The correlation between out of stock care package items and their sodium concentration. 3. The correlation between suicides and distance from home.	how lonely your [splendor] the rhyme between [splendor] and rage a small anger and a large [splendor] no [luster] quite so eponymous no [pageantry] that can out live us
In a mass surveillance state in which we are all internet stars. I look dutifully for your wound	GPS ankle monitors establish patterns of movement, length and frequency of travel to determine punishment for departure from the mean	30%: expanded definition of solitude and let us not forgive any of it. 40%: interrogation and its limits of ascension. 30%: The committee declares a center to your abatement— pressed by & by.

beauty proper and minor.

Due to circumstances of things relating to "distance" and "removal" and "access" and "interest,"

beyond what words mean anyways,

the minor aesthete or

        the longest road

The private for profit corrections company GEO Group is publicly listed as a real estate investment trust which has re-written into the congressional record the corporate definition of land and ownership.

I am working on getting my kids home. None of this is in my own words. I have not spoken yet. But I'm looking: [Nonetheless a wreckage, the committee declares a trembling, the unbroken vessel of September.]

---

toward text that contains no solace, let it live in its own idea of isolation, let no image be spared in our terrible imagination of it.

Risk assessment prediction software determines bail and/or amount and in some cases, parole.

The algorithm assesses likelihood of flight risk or repeat offense.

(detained minor class notes: "Epistolary, symbolism: one thing meaning something else —> metaphor. Why build a house around a dying crow? Why not help the creature instead?)

*** Plato said we discern color by projecting matter onto the objects we look at***

I part my beloved's hair
the moon declares its particulars

Sappho had it right though,
goddamn did she have it right.

The poem in which the word
"cage" is never used

It was morning when ICE raided my brother's home and detained him. He is studying computer science to design more effective tracking algorithms for @Twitter.

I place your right palm on my head.
        Said *I will*
        Said *another name*
        Said *necessary project of*
        retaliation
A preferred language that objects to all forms of witness
I own Said *anger*
refused even the
intentions of trust
and confess a heart may be two
questions in Spanish.

	a quantifiable change that can be documented measured funded to prove to promise	CAP (criminal alien program) has collapsed the avenues of jurisdiction between immigration enforcement and criminal enforcement.	[Keep the minor] #AbolishICE #FamiliesBelongTogether #ACAB #TwoHouseholds #BothAlikeInDignity #InFairVerona [Their alternate forms of citizenship]
	the interviewer asks about bridges	Per conditions of release, my father is required to answer a call every third Sunday of the month at exactly 8am and speak his name into the AI voice detection software which has categorized every nuanced morpheme and decibel calibration of his name. If his utterance does not match, an agent will be in touch shortly. My father answers and says his name slowly as if it's not his.	…in which the word… In the absence of its **bewilderment** Stripe after unforgiving stripe How in one hand the film In the other the **remedy**, And its derelict vision, A nearby future, As if the shape denies its circumstance We watch everything **burn** as it should A trembling, an easy way home
Poetry is stupid and I want to die *(1)		Googled all prisons in California and Google suggests if I'm looking for "best federal prisons in California" (four out of five stars) Googled the word rapt and felt a sigh of relief to see that it was actually a word and that I had used it correctly.	{Detained Minor 2, field notes: "I wish you could bring better books…shoot out like big jack…it's a robbery, it's taxes, it's a story"}* Redacted. In anticipation of your spectral victimhood : one clover, one bee, and revery

---

*(1) "I can give you no language that will free the child from her cage, make no meaning that un-floods the world, no verse that can un-fire the bullet." —Vanessa Angélica Villarreal

Roque Raquel Salas Rivera

La promiscuidad tan indeseable

En 1934,
      la inmigración del campo
llevó a la formación
      de la Corte Nocturna,
para procesar
      de noche y de día.
Los niños se enviaban a Mayagüez,
      las niñas a Ponce,
las mujeres a Arecibo.
      Algunas pasaban
por el Oso Blanco
      (Paula, empleada doméstica,
natural de Vieques). En el 1939,
      el primer caso de corrupción,
que llega a lo que se llega:
      irregularidades en el manejo
y desembolso de fondos,
      irregularidades en
la investigación del propio gobierno.
      Ese mismo año,
la cárcel se supera. La más moderna
      de su época, pocos salen
con oficio, pocos salen, con
      sentencias más largas
y el rigor. Ya para el 1940,
      dejaron el afán reformista,
pasan a *donde sea posible, donde*
      esté disponible, si se puede
auto-sostener. El Procurador General
      da informes al grano.
Cenex cumple su sexto año
      y se sabe que hay una guerra
mundial, como se sabe de todo

        fuera de la norma, porque
paran los rumores de expansión,
        de una nueva ala. Entraba
menos gente durante la guerra,
        también nada mejoraba,
pero comenzaron a llegar más.
        Después que se ganó
o perdió lo que se iba a a a a a
        directo a la boca del oso:
los delitos más graves, las sentencias
        más largas y después de
la guerra y durante la guerra, menos
        comida, menos ropa.
Aún así, dicen que por ser más grande
        era mejor. Ya ven que tienen biblias
y misa en el patio interior. La más moderna
        de la modernidad.
El Procurador General Enrique Campos del Toro,
        militar, humanista autocrítico,
sus palabras tan hondas como cualquier
        calabozo: *El preso no se le reconoce calor*
humano alguno. Para recapitular, *En nuestras cárceles,*
        en nuestra cárcel, se hacinan de todos tipos,
los delincuentes, todos viviendo en la promiscuidad
        tan indeseable.[4] Cuando usa la palabra
ocio, se refiere al tiempo. Según el General
        existe un exceso temporal,
un exceso táctil. Su solución es simple,
        aumentar los talleres, triplicar
la producción. Las reformas aliviaban

---

4 "El preso no se le reconoce calor humano alguno. Cometido el delito, es sentenciado y se le arroja en una prisión como si fuera una peste o un residuo social que no merece más consideración. En esta forma el Estado consuma la obra de degradación y exterminio de ese ser humano de cuyo delito, acaso, la sociedad misma es responsable." Enrique Campos del Toro, Informe del Procurador General, 1946.

              la promiscuidad, acompañadas
por nuevas ilegalidades. Ahora jugar
              bolita y bolipool, ahora la paga
por ciertos servicios no regulados,
              como ser de Loíza, nacido,
criado y arrestado. Pasan las décadas,
              todos aumentan, todo disminuye.
Una tal Helen Hooker denuncia la falta
              que le hacen en un mundo de
faltas y fallos, pero dice algo común
              e increíble, que Cenex no deja
de repetirse de noche: *tremendo esfuerzo por
              tapar el cielo con la mano.*[5]
El cielo, con la mano no es imposible.
              Cada día, las manos construyen cielos.
El cielo es cosa de planificación,
              pero si atrapas unas manos,
aprendes a pescar nubes.

---

5   Helen V. Tooker, "El presidio tiene 4 serias deficiencias," *El Mundo*, 29 de octubre de 1950. p.1

Roque Raquel Salas Rivera

Such Undesirable Promiscuity

In 1934,
    migration from the fields
led to the formation
    of the Nocturnal Court,
to process
    night and day.
Boys were sent to Mayagüez,
    girls to Ponce,
women to Arecibo.
    Some passed
through el Oso Blanco
    (Paula, domestic worker,
originally from Vieques). In 1939,
    the first case of corruption,
that leads to what it does:
    irregularities in the management
and disbursement of funds,
    irregularities in
the government's self-investigation.
    That same year,
the prison self-exceeds. The most
    modern of its era, few leave
with new trades, few leave, with
    sentences longer
and more rigor. By 1940,
    they quit all reformist drive,
moving on to *wherever possible,*
    wherever available, if it can
self-sustain. The Attorney General
    gives no-nonsense reports.
Cenex spends his sixth year
    and knows there is a world
war, like he knows about all

        things outside the norm, because
expansion rumors have stopped,
        no new wing. Less people
came in during the war,
        also, nothing improved,
but later came more.
        After it was won or lost,
whatever we e e e e nt
        directly to the bear's mouth:
the felonies, more serious, the servings
        longer and after the
war, and during the war, less
        food, less clothes.
Even so, they say because it is bigger,
        it is better. You can see there are
bibles and mass in the inner patio. The most
        modern of all modernity.
The Attorney General Enrique Campos del Toro,
        military officer, self-critical humanist,
his words as deep as any
        dungeon: *The inmate does not recognize*
any human heat. To recapitulate, *in our prisons,*
        in our prison, all sorts overcrowd,
delinquents, all living in such undesirable
        promiscuity.[6] When he uses the word
idleness, he means time. According to the Attorney
        General, there is a temporal excess,
a tactile excess. His solution is simple,
        increase the workshops, triplicate
production. Reforms alleviated

---

6 "The inmate does not recognize any human heat. Once the crime is committed, he is sentenced, and thrown in a prison as if he were a plague or a social residue that does not deserve more consideration. This is how the State consummates the work of degrading and exterminating this human being for whose crime, in any case, that very society is responsible." Enrique Campos del Toro, Attorney General's Report, 1946.

        promiscuity, accompanied
by new illegalities. Now to play
        pool, now to pay for
certain unregulated services, like being
        from Loíza, born, raised, and arrested.
The decades pass, everyone increases,
        everything diminishes.
Until, one Helen Hooker denounces lack
        in a world full of lacks and failures,
but says something incredible and
        common, that Cenex keeps
mumbling at night: *a great effort to cover*
        the sky with one hand.[7]
See, the sky, with one hand is not impossible.
        Every day, hands build skies.
The sky just takes planning,
        but if you trap some hands,
you can learn to catch clouds.

---

7 Helen Tooker, "The prison has 4 serious deficiencies," *El Mundo*, October 28, 1950. p. 1

VII

Like a Hammer: The Forgotten Impoverished

Nikky Finney

Black Boy with Cow: A Still Life

Still life can be a celebration of material pleasures such as food and wine, or often a warning of ephemerality of these pleasures and the brevity of human life.

—Definition of "Still Life," Tate Galleries Website

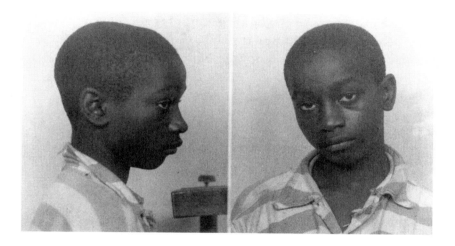

On the occasion of George J. Stinney Jr., fourteen, the youngest to die in the electric chair in these United States of America, commissioned by the University of Arizona Poetry Center's Art for Justice grant.

BEFORE

We stand before the bowl of his eyes, no fruit in the picture, the curve and curl of his desires waiting to be filled, he looks sideways back at us, we could fill his bowl with hundreds of his black boy sketches, airplanes, automobiles, at the very

Least, at the very least, we could fill it with his cow, with
his penitentiary record, George J. Stinney Jr., Age: fourteen,
Height: five feet, Weight: ninety-five pounds, Hair: Negro,
Eyes: dark maroon. Home: Alcolu, rural South Carolina.

In 1944, there are Black churches and white churches, Black
schools, white schools, white girls, Black boys. There are railroad
tracks. There are always railroad tracks when there are white
girls and Black boys living two hundred feet from each other.

This is the Jim Crow South. If you are Black and riding in a
car please make sure the car you are passing does not contain
white people. This is the cotton law of the cotton land. If you
are walking do not walk near or brush against a white person

Who is also walking. Touching a white person is illegal.
If you are lost and need to ask a white person how to get home be
inclined to stay lost. Do not ask for help with N-S-E-W, you
could be arrested for asking a white person for directions.

Remember, the eyes of (any) white person are always out of
range. This is the story of a Black boy with a cow and his
pencils. His still life. His Black boy no-way-out life. This is
the still life of George J. Stinney Jr. of Alcolu.

Thursday, March 23, 1944: Two girls, white, were last seen
on one bike, out looking for maypops. Friday, March 24,
1944: Two bodies of two girls, Betty June Binnicker, eleven,
Mary Emma Thames, seven, are found side by side, on their

Backs, in three inches of water, the bike they were seen riding
the day before has been laid across their bodies like a paperweight.
A report comes in. George Junius Stinney Jr., fourteen, is the
last person to see the girls. Does this mean last to *look* at the

Girls, who were out looking for maypops and stopped to ask
where they were? The census of the Jim Crow South does show

there were mystics alive in 1944, white people who saw things that Black people did not. The girls stopped to ask George

And his sister, Aimé, if they had seen any maypops and if so —where? In the Jim Crow South, Black children know that one-word answers are best and make for fewer bruises. Black children are taught this in utero. Aimé answers for them both,

No. A maypop is the fruit of the passion flower. When it turns from bright green to orange it is sweet, succulent, ready to eat. When you step on a maypop before it is ready it makes a popping sound. The bodies of the girls were found on the Black side

Of town. Beaten to death with a railroad tie—or hammer. Two skulls smashed, two hymens intact, the eleven-year-old has a bruise. They think there is semen on her thigh. We must now put the word "semen" in the bowl beside the cow. The language

Of rape has entered the community switchboard. All operators are busy and not standing by. The bowl which only had a cow and the boy's drawing pencils now has the word "semen" but not the word "Proof": "Semen" is a word that stretches back

Hundreds of years to that great camp meeting where skins of different color were measured and weighed on a scale along with various-size craniums all inched and ranked by protractor, sun dial, caliper, and numerical tape. The word-of-mouth,

Over-the-fence, long-playing record that the operators are now spinning wildly is the very reason there are railroad tracks in Southern towns with different people with different-colored skin living on different sides. One side of town can't play the song

Enough. The other side is hurrying to get out of town before the song stops playing. There will never be evidence to support the song that is played on high repeat. The repeat-song is now and forever one of the Republic's greatest hits. It has now been

Placed in the bowl with the Black boy and his cow and what
they believe is semen. This is the Black boy's still life. The man
who found the girls says there was not much blood around the
ditch itself. He adds that it looks as if they were killed somewhere

Else. But no one ever looks for somewhere else. Because all
the memorable catchy high notes of the long-playing song have
now been memorized alongside barrel clicks. Before George
Jr. was told to take off his Saturday T-shirt and blue jeans,

The clothes he had just walked the family cow in, he was told
to put on their blue prison stripes, and turn forward, and turn
to the side, to reveal the true colors of his maroon eyes. He was
in the seventh grade. A good student who routinely told his mother,

A cook, in the Jim Crow South, that he wanted to be an artist
when he grew up. So for practice he drew airplanes and automobiles
on pieces of scrap paper. Planes and autos fly away and move fast.
Do you think young George thought these were machines that

Might help him leave the Jim Crow South? The bowl holding
these boy-with-Negro-hair desires will be collected over and
over again. The still life of Black boys will be the Republic's
largest collection plate. Four XL men, not with Negro hair,

Arrive at the house that is owned by the lumber company where
the father works. Aimé, George's youngest sister, sees the men
and runs to hide in the chicken coop. Surrounded by warm eggs
and cackling hens. She watches as George's drawing hands are

Handcuffed. She sees the men, who live on the other side of
the tracks, walk her brother outside and put him in the back
of the XL black car. Sees their guns and billy clubs. Sees that
she has accidentally broken some of the eggs her family needs

To live. Aimé is seven years old. Idolizes George. George calls
her his Shadow. Seventy years after hiding in the chicken coop

she will remember yelling for her brother, *Oh George where are you going?* George Junius Stinney Jr., five feet tall and ninety-five

Pounds, is taken away. There are no witnesses to the murders. The only physical evidence ever written down is "Negro hair" and "maroon eyes." This is what spins around and around the record player in Alcolu every night until dawn. Aimé's screams

For her brother are finally put inside of his bowl. George Junius Stinney Jr., fourteen, dreamer of all things with wheels and wings, who once had a still life in motion now only has a still life. He is questioned and more, with no attorney and no family

Present. Half the night, in a dark small room with XL men with silk hair holding billy clubs and dangling pistols, from the other side of the tracks. He confesses to the crime. Well, they *say* he confesses just like they *believe* there is semen. A signed confession

Will never be found because one will never be given. There will only be the word of four XL men against one fourteen-year-old boy who would give anything to see his mother and walk his cow again. The boy with Negro hair & maroon eyes is charged with

Capital murder. The confession changes to fit the prosecution. The confession changes to fit the weather. The murder weapon is changed at will. First it is a hammer then it is a railroad tie. Anything at all is changed in whatever manner serves the

Cotton law of the land and the Greatest Hit ever made and the bowl that rests in the middle of the velvet canvas boasts the ephemerality of life. Materials normally arranged in such a bowl—oranges, apples, roses, muscadines, plums, Sweet

William—are not in George's bowl. A cow, a few pencils, what looks like semen, and a sister's last scream for her brother are. In the Jim Crow South. One-word answers are best. Two at the most. Black children of the deepest South are taught,

Then and now, shortly after the afterbirth has dried behind
their ears, the two words that might keep them alive, *Yes suh*.
But not even *Yes suh* is foolproof. There was never a transcript.
No written confession. Only the long-playing song of the

Black boy who looked at two white girls who were already
out looking for fruit that had already popped. An appeal is
made to the governor of South Carolina for clemency.
The governor of South Carolina responds in writing.

Finally, something has been written down:
*It may be interesting for you to know that
Stinney killed the smaller girl to rape the larger
one. Then he killed the larger girl and raped*

*Her dead body. Twenty minutes later
he returned and attempted to rape her
again but her body was too cold. All of
this he admitted.*   Liar.

The governor is lying and the popular lyrics of the
best-selling song have made its way to the Governor's
mansion in South Carolina. No confession. Nothing written
down. But mystics truly believe in each other and George's

Court-appointed lawyer is busy running for a statehouse
seat and needs every vote. He does nothing to defend George.
He calls no witnesses and at the end of the day waves to
the prosecuting team who are his neighbors on the other

Side of the tracks. He calls no police to the stand and sits
quietly at his table for all of the ten minutes it takes the all
white male jury to return their verdict. The fourteen-year
old, known for getting his friends to sing along to the radio

In the yard near the chicken coop, after he has walked then
watered the family cow: the ninety-five-pounder who wanted

to finish the seventh grade so that be might one day be known
for his fast cars and airplanes, is ordered to the electric chair.

No appeal is ever filed by the attorney running for the seat
at the statehouse. George never goes home again. He is put
into a cell with an older man. Johnny. For eighty-three days,
while George waits to die, Johnny is his only family. George's

Fourteen-year-old mind keeps wondering what it will mean
to be electrocuted and *Why would someone want to kill me
for something I don't know anything about?* His fourteen-year
old mind, that liked to watch cars and airplanes fly, that has

Been taught right from wrong, fenders from wings, wonders.
Why would they charge me with something I didn't do? This
is what George asks Johnny. Johnny is twice George's age,
with Negro hair and maroon eyes, and no bowl to his name

And no answer to give the boy about to die. There are many
more generations behind them both, Black boys with still
lives. Their still lives will wait in bowls painted with iron
& electricity, provided and financed by the state and the nation.

But in 1944, a reporter from *The State* newspaper in South
Carolina wrote that George J. Stinney Jr. was walked to his
death with a Bible underneath his arm. He reported that the
fourteen-year-old was orderly. Polite. Obeying the men from

The other side of the tracks without incident. Did he walk like
a boy back in school? Headed to the library to return a book?
He reported that George J. Stinney Jr. was made to sit on the
Bible that he was made to carry into the death chamber.

The electric chair was made for men and George was just
a boy. A boy with a mother, father, two sisters, two brothers,
and one cow waiting for him back at home. The reporter
reported that the guards had great difficulty strapping the

Small fourteen-year-old into the chair. He later reports the electrodes were too big for George's legs. When the switch is flipped the first time, 2,400 volts of man-made electricity cause an earthquake, man-size convulsions shake and roll,

Knocking the large mask off his boy-size head, exposing his tearful face, singeing his Negro hair and sending his maroon eyes all the way to the back of his skull. Two more jolts of 2,400 volts of electricity take four more minutes to run their

Slow lightning storm and category 7 hurricane through his empty bowl of a body before the boy who loved to draw flying things and long-winged cars is pronounced dead. His still life over. The air fills with hot comb hair & Black boy skin.

AFTER

Seventy years pass before anyone will give the Stinney
family the only thing they have ever wanted. *We do not
want an apology*, they tell the newspapers. *We want coram
nobis. It's the best we can get.* Coram nobis: Mistakes

*Were made. We petition the state of South Carolina to
hear our plea. January 21, 2014, Sumter; South Carolina.*
The court hearing begins at 11:00 but I am in the parking
lot by 9:00. It's a one-hour drive from Columbia to Sumter,

Where, in 1944, George J. Stinney Jr., found guilty
of capital murder, was electrocuted. Here, in Sumter, is where
George and I were both raised. In 1944 he was fourteen.
In 1944, my father was thirteen. News of the coram nobis

Hearing has been swirling hot in the South Carolina air for
months. Daddy is eighty-three now. George J. Stinney Jr.
should be eighty-four but he is not. I am waiting my turn
at the metal detector. My journal book is deep in my bag.

There are three purple pens in my bag that I tested
for strength and longevity earlier this morning. From the
look of the line at the metal detector the courtroom will
be packed. Most of the people waiting with me are Black.

We say *Good morning* with a clear and deliberate sadness.
We know why we are here. Most of the policemen and
women checking us through to the courtroom are Black.
My bag is slowly searched. My journal book pulled out,

Turned over, opened, pages leafed & thumbed through.
My phone is taken. No cell phones in the courtroom.
I can pick it up when I leave. I tell her I need my pens.
She tells me I cannot write in the courtroom during the

Hearing. Unless I am a reporter. I tell her I am a reporter.
She changes her mind and tells me I can keep my pens
because pens aren't what they are looking for. She says,
Pens aren't dangerous. I walk in the courtroom looking

Around. Four members of the Stinney family are directly
across from me. I get up from my seat, walk over, say
Good morning. They nod and say *Good morning* back.
I go back to where I first sat down. There is a sadness in

The eyes of the family that will take me the rest of my life
to move off my heart. I look up and I realize I am diagonally
across from the portrait of Daddy, Sumter Circuit County
Judge Ernest A. Finney Jr., mad crusader against the death

Penalty, who presided in this courtroom for two decades,
in this Sumter town, where I was raised, after George Junius
Stinney Jr., was electrocuted for having Negro hair and
maroon eyes. I have not seen Daddy's portrait in twenty-five

Years. I remember coming home from college to the unveiling
of this Black man wearing his monumental black robe in a
town that still honored the Confederacy. Daddy's eyes hold
me in place. The courtroom has filled quickly. The bailiff

Announces no recording devices are allowed. He tells us if
we are caught recording we will be fined $500 then escorted
out. There is a Black woman sheriff on one side of the room.
A Black man sheriff at the back. The solicitor is my brother,

Ernest A. Finney III. The faces of justice have changed.
The mind and heart of justice has not. One portrait of one
Black judge officially hung in a courtroom does not dismantle
ten generations of discrimination and injustice that has long

Hung over this town, city, and state. While we wait for the judge
to enter people behind me are whispering their personal

stories about what it was like to grow up here. We are of
different generations but all our stories seem to hurt the same.

Being seen as fear and trouble is the brick and pebble of each
story. The perception of being a person of trouble, aimed for
trouble, because of what we always come in the door wearing.
Negro hair and maroon eyes. There is more trouble for some.

Less trouble for others. I look across the aisle. The two men
in the Stinney family pew have now folded their arms in tight.
The Stinney women are quiet. This is not a church but the
wooden seats in the courthouse have a certain resemblance.

This institution of law. That institution of religion. It is not
Sunday but it is 11 o'clock, still that most segregated of
hours. Two attorneys, young, white, with seashell faces and
silk hair, hired by the Stinney family, have agreed to work

Pro bono to seek this writ of coram nobis. They have taken
their place at the defense table, directly in front of Daddy's
portrait, to the left of my oldest brother, the county solicitor.
The judge is young, white, and female. All month in the

South Carolina newspapers she has been called courageous,
a maverick even. She does not have to hear this case. After
all it has been seventy years. She does not have to allow for
this hearing. After all this is still South Carolina. Still the

Deep South. Jim Crow has gray hair but is not dead. The
Confederate flag still flies over the statehouse, still bumps
the backsides of pickup trucks, denim jackets, and motor-
cycles. She addresses the court as soon as she sits:

*Not much was done for this child and I am not here to rule on
his guilt or innocence. As far as I am concerned he could have
committed these crimes. I am here only to rule on whether he received
a fair trial.* Miss Julia Bowen, civil rights matriarch,

There on the front lines back in the old old days of old-school
organizing for people with Negro hair and maroon eyes,
lowers her head. Both of us have been kicked in the stomach
by the judge's *impartial* words. We are not impartial. Our

Pew of the courtroom wants less law and more empathy.
She pulls out her handkerchief to touch the corners of her
eyes, just as the maverick judge adds, *We now have safeguards
against this ever happening again.* The hands of all the Black

People on my row with Negro hair and maroon eyes lift
and levitate in disbelief, secretly, below the backs of the hard
chairs we are all sitting in. We catch and hold each other's
fingers in midflight. Our hands are strung together in a

West African herringbone weave. The bailiff turns to look
at our row, giving us his eye. *Defense counsel, this is your
motion so make your plea. Your Honor; George Stinney Jr.
was fourteen years old. He was the youngest person ever

Executed in this country. We believe wrongfully convicted
and wrongly executed. A writ of coram nobis is requested,
Your Honor; when someone like George J. Stinney Jr. falls
through the cracks of the law as we assert he did. In addition,*

*Your Honor; as further evidence, the discovery of hundreds
of letters of support for George J. Stinney Jr. by people across
the country asking for him to receive due process.* The young
lawyer with golden hair like his mother goes on to tell how

Two South Carolina governors, long after the one who refused
to commute George Stinney's death sentence, spoke out,
calling the case a long moment of *shame and disgrace* for the
state of South Carolina. He reports that another governor went

So far as to say, *This is a moment that will never die.*
I clear my throat and turn the page of my journal as loud

as I can. The bailiff puts his fingers to his lips. The lawyer
states for the record of the court the crime, *how the bodies*

Of the two young girls were found on March 23, 1944.
How did I miss this? Daddy's thirteenth birthday. My eyes
lift and fly across the room to his judicious face, his Negro
hair is backlit, his maroon eyes bright and shining. My father

Was thirteen years old and George J. Stinney Jr. was fourteen
years old. In 1944, my father, Ernest A. Finney Jr., abandoned
his cow in Virginia and made his way to South Carolina riding
shotgun in the passenger seat of his father's long emerald

Green car with silver wings. My grandfather, Ernest A. Finney
Sr., had taken a new job as dean of students at Claflin College,
a historically Black college in South Carolina. George J.
Stinney Jr. was the son of George J. Stinney Sr., a man who

Owned one cow and could not read or write. This still life
that I am drawing in this courtroom of my father and George
Stinney's father is clearly about Negro hair and maroon eyes
but also clearly about isolation and poverty and who gets

To drive away and who does not. The solicitor stands up.
*Your Honor, the State of South Carolina maintains that
George J. Stinney Jr. was guilty and deserved the death penalty.*
My legs try their best to bolt. The bailiff moves and stands at

The end of the aisle nearest me. He can feel me rising to face
my brother. But I do not look his way or stand. I have not come
to make a scene with the state of South Carolina or in front of
the brother I dearly love. I have come to be George J. Stinney's

Reporter. The eyes and ears that James Baldwin spoke of fifty
years before, *Only the Poet can tell us what it is like to be human.
Only the Poet can tell us what it is like for anyone who gets to
this planet to survive it.* I bear the weight of my pen all the way

PART VII: LIKE A HAMMER

Down and my brother, as solicitor, continues. *Your Honor, this is about standing and timeliness. This case is seventy years old.*
It is clear the defendant had a clear constitutional right to counsel and that he had counsel. A writ of habeas corpus is the only other

Remedy that exists. *Habeas corpus,* to bring the body forward. The defense objects: *Coram nobis, Your Honor. Your Honor, the state's hands are dirty.* I write *dirty* then underscore it hard in my journal book. *At the very least,* he says it twice, *at the very*

Least, *the state must say: A mistake was made.* I am scribbling uncontrollably and loudly again. The bailiff makes his move to the end of my row again. He knows my brother and my father. He does not know me. I write: *The solicitor is wrong*

And the defense too nice. Bring it. Bring habeas corpus into this already burning ring of fire. Bring all five feet of his Black boy body out of his unmarked grave and back into the sweet magnolia air of South Carolina. Let all see the body that his

Sister and mother and father could not recognize in the casket seventy years ago. Bring the Black boy's scorched black body into this room. Let us see the bowl of soft eyes of the ninety five-pounder whose last act as a fourteen-year-old, who loved

To draw, was trying to figure out how best to situate his tiny self on top of the Holy Bible. It awkwardly sat between him and his wooden chair so that the electric current of the state could officially reach up high enough in the chaotic air of his

Wondering *why me* mind and burn him to a Black boy crisp. *The state's hands are not dirty,* I want to scream, *they are foaming with blood.* At the very least. The state walked a child to the electric chair with no evidence other than his Negro hair

And maroon eyes. His father could not defend or save him and was forced to sacrifice fighting out loud for him in order

to save the rest of his family. George Stinney Sr. left Alcolu,
South Carolina, and went north. My purple pen is moving like

A hammer across the page. My heart is pounding through my
chest when Katherine Stinney-Robinson, seventy-nine, sister of
George J. Stinney Jr., takes the stand. *Do you solemnly swear. . .
the whole truth. . .* Her voice is not frail. *I do.* Her eyes turn.

What do you remember about South Carolina in 1944?
Nothing good. And may I say, she clarifies, *a maypop is a
fruit, not flower. More like a lemon.* She was nine. Idolized
her brother. *He liked to draw,* she says again. Her eyes clear.

Seventy years later. She and her brother should be growing
old together (with Daddy). Our West African herringbone
hands tighten. She says the day before he was arrested it
was same as usual. The day he was arrested it all went haywire.

(Did George speak to the two girls?) *No. He just looked.
I was his shadow. We had a three-room house. Somebody
would've noticed if he had on bloody clothes. He didn't
have any blood on his clothes.* (How many changing clothes

Do you think we had, her eyes ask him. *Some people can
just change their clothes whenever they want,* her feet want
to say. *We didn't have clothes like that,* her folded hands
remind.) *He never came back. Some men came and took him.*

*My father came home and took us to my grandmother's
house.* (No one came to ask you any questions?) *No. He was
just there one minute and then he was gone.* I write *Poof*
in my journal book. May it please the court. *One Black boy*

Goes Poof must be added to the bowl. While she answers
his ancient questions, I want to write something about what
people with Negro hair and maroon eyes have to endure
after the child they love is sat upon the Holy Bible before

Being sat upon their electric chair. The long-drawn trauma
of a people with Negro hair and maroon eyes to endure the
law of their land. The long-drawn trauma of not being on the
voting list or not being on the jury list. Of having to protect

your one cow or not having a car with wings to drive out
of the bloody South or not being able to read or own your
one room of a house or the long act of intimidation by the
great billy clubs of America. Of being fourteen and put in the

Backseat of the car, that up until that handcuffed moment,
you had drawn with great dream precision of being behind
the wheel of one day. The terror of counting fifteen hundred
white people mystics of the Jim Crow South outside the

Courthouse calling your name, a name that after ten minutes
is found guilty and sent to the electric chair with the Good
Book as your booster seat. My pages are heavy links in a
long chain as I turn them. The bailiff hears me and moves

To the end of my aisle. There is a pathologist's report.
My brother glances over his shoulder towards me. Daddy
doesn't move. I don't look his way. It is not an autopsy
report. There was no autopsy. It is not a forensic report.

It is only an external exam. The family doctor was called.
Whose family gets to have a family doctor? I wonder this
with my head down. *No defensive wounds,* says the man
reading the pathologist's report. He had to be large to do

This kind of damage. There should have been blood at the
scene. No photographs were taken. There are so many blood
vessels in the scalp. Unusual that there was not a lot of blood
on the ground. Daddy's portrait is one hundred feet in front

Of me. He believed in the law like nobody's business. I
whisper to him during the recess. *Daddy, this thing called*

law is sticky. I remember him walking through the house at night with a cigarette in one hand and law books in the other:

The law works, girl. Daddy, I know you believe that the law works. But the law does not always work. The law is not the flower you told me it was. It's more like a fruit, like a maypop and sometimes when the law is stepped on there is

A loud popping sound, for some of us. Daddy, the law you love so much can hide behind so many other things, like the texture of a boy's hair and the color of his eyes. Daddy, the law makes people with Negro hair and maroon eyes and one cow wait past

Forever for just a sliver of truth. And after that nothing really changes. Negro-hair people get the jobs that silky-haired people used to have. But the seesaw rule books are the same. Status quo. Who you know. One cow versus who owns the

Slaughterhouse. His fourteen-year-old brain knew he was going to die. He died wondering why anyone would want to hurt him, accuse him of something he did not do. He obeyed the law and took his seat on top of the Bible he was taught to believe in.

His still life never filled in. He died with chaos & confusion pounding his heart. His family continued to raise the other children to the tune of this same chaos and confusion. *We had an open casket,* his sister testified. *He was burned so badly.*

Hardly recognizable. An unmarked grave, so no one would ever hurt him again, she said. The cow sold. The three-room house shut. The chicken coop empty. No one in the Stinney family ever wanted to hear the word "maypop" ever again.

The violence done to children whom the state has been taught to fear, since the day they were born, does not go *Poof,* does not disappear after the state burns them alive. It does not go away or disappear below in the ground water. What the state

Has done lives on. It floats in the air like a fine powder that
follows us and falls on all our bare arms and shoulders. It follows
us to the beach and to retirement parties. The state not only
murders the fourteen-year-old sitting on the Bible but smokes

The whole family. There is a bolt of long-range electricity shot
through the mother, the father, the brother, the shadow of the sister,
the cow. There was no evidence. There was only a country's top-
ten hit memorized by heart and whistled into soda and beer cans.

The people who lied have now died. The man who killed the girls,
who was never looked for, is dead now too. People with Negro
hair and maroon eyes still wait every day for anybody who killed
or kidnapped one of their own to die first so the truth can finally

Come out. *A writ of coram nobis is the best we can get.* The court
adjourns and the maverick judge announces her decision and we
are supposed to be delighted by her twenty-first-century courage.
The conviction is overturned and the family agrees to sit for a family

Portrait seventy years after the fact. The camera shows that everybody
is missing. The mother with Negro hair keeps looking around for
her boy. She herringbones his empty chair with her arm. The sister
says they are happy that her brother's name has finally been cleared.

She is eighty years old now and can die. There is a fine alabaster
powder on all our hands as we keep holding on. He will never
disappear from our bowl. The boy who kept looking behind him
in the courtroom that day, looking for his father to walk in the door,

Touch his shoulder, take him home, is our son with soft brown cow
eyes and his short-lived life will always be the story of a boy who
arrived to the great land of fast wheels, shiny fenders, and plentiful
wings and was burned alive.

READING AND DISCUSSION GUIDE

Rachael Zafer

Educators, activists, poetry readers: Looking to engage this book more deeply? This guide is designed for classrooms, study groups, book clubs, and individual readers interested in reflection, study, and action. It serves as an invitation to think deeply about the carceral state and to envision a world without surveillance, without policing, and without prisons. Our guide includes companion questions for each section of *Like a Hammer*, and a resources section with additional tools, organizations, and further reading.

Visit **haymarketbooks.org/books/2438-like-a-hammer** for the full, free reading and discussion guide.

I. TIME RULES THIS EMPIRE: WHERE CLOCKS STAND STILL

1. How do poets in this section experience time? What was your experience of time as you read this section?

2. How does the United States prison industrial complex function as an empire (a political unit with a large number of peoples under one ruler with total authority)? How is power written about throughout this section—who has it, who enforces it, who wants it, and how does it move?

II. BE CAREFUL HOW YOU SPEAK ABOUT RAINBOWS: BEAUTY & GRACE

1. What are some moments of beauty described by poets throughout this section? How do these moments contrast with descriptions of hardship and isolation?

2. How does Eduardo Martinez's poem "A.G.A.M." explore immigration and borders? How has language been used as a tool to create and

spread divisions in the United States? How is the prison industrial complex intertwined with immigration?

III. THE BILL IS PAST DUE: THE HUSTLE

1. How does this section reference the poverty-to-prison pipeline? Where do you notice poets writing about the racial identities of people impacted by incarceration?

2. Learn more about cash bail and excessive bail funds. How are these practices used to keep people in jails as they await trial? Who is most impacted by these practices? Who profits from them? Is there a local bail fund in your community that provides bail to people in need? How can you support or amplify their work?

VI. THE NAKEDNESS DARK DEMANDS: SURVEILLANCE AND SHAPESHIFTING

1. What did you experience looking at the images in Vanessa Angélica Villarreal's poem "Architect III"? How does Villarreal draw connections between people incarcerated in the United States in the eighteenth century and people incarcerated today?

VII. LIKE A HAMMER: THE FORGOTTEN IMPOVERISHED

1. Look closely at the photograph of George Stinney Jr. included with Nikky Finney's "Black Boy with Cow, A Still Life." What do Stinney's eyes communicate? How is he described throughout the poem?

Rachael Zafer is a writer, organizer, graphic designer, and the author of discussion guides for over thirty books including *We Do This 'Til We Free Us* by Mariame Kaba and *Abolition for the People*, edited by Colin Kaepernick. You can view her discussion guides at www.rachaelzafer.com.

ACKNOWLEDGMENTS

Reginald Dwayne Betts, "Blood History" appears on Poets.org (2019), Poems.com (January 10, 2020), Issue 230 of the *Paris Review* (2019), and AlisonMcGhee.com (June 20, 2020).

Natalie Diaz, "Under Correction I" appears in an article on the website Terremoto, February 3, 2023.

Tongo Eisen-Martin, "Knees Next to Their Wallets" appears in *Blood on the Fog: Pocket Poets Series No. 6*. (City Lights, 2021).

Nikky Finney, "Black Boy with Cow: A Still Life" appears in *Love Child's Hotbed of Occasional Poetry: Poems & Artifacts* (Northwestern University Press, 2020). Republished by permission.

Kennedy A. Gisege, "Break from Madness" and "Scattered Like Yellow Feathers" appear in *Men Matters Online Journal*, Issue #4, June 2022.

Randall Horton, ": .Or. This *Malus* Thing Never to Be Confused with Justice" appears in *Poetry*, May 2019.

Ada Limón, "What Is Caged Is Also Kept from Us" appears in *The Cincinnati Review*, 17.2 (Fall 2020).

Christopher Malec, "Order's Up" is published on the Exchange for Change website, 2022.

Nicole Sealey, "Pages Thirteen to Twenty-One" appears in *The Ferguson Report: An Erasure*. (Knopf, 2023).

Evie Shockley, "Can't Unsee" appears in *suddenly we* (Wesleyan University Press, 2023).

Sin à Tes Souhaits, "TRAP noun. \'trap\" appears in the *Sun* (November 2020); an earlier version of "Sometimes I Wonder If God Really Fuck with Me Like That" was previously published in the *Rumpus* (2019).

Vanessa Angélica Villarreal, a version of "Architect 3" appears as "table {border-collapse:collapse;}" in the *Nation*, June 23, 2022

Candace Williams, "A Good Cop" appears in *Already Felt: Poems in Revolution & Bounty* (Raptor Press, 2021).

CONTRIBUTORS

Hanif Abdurraqib is a writer from the east side of Columbus, Ohio.

Rhionna (Rhae) Anderson is an incarcerated individual who enjoys writing in her free time. When she is not writing you can find her on the rec yard working out. She is a free spirit who loves the Lord.

Brian Batchelor is a poet and artist currently working on a chapbook of illuminated poems. He is a member of the Stillwater Writer's Collective and has been an avid participant in workshops taught by writers from the Minnesota Prison Writing Workshop. Batchelor was born in 1983 in the tiny town of Washington, D.C. When he doesn't have a paint brush in hand, a nice cheap Bic pen takes its place. Albert Camus said it best: "A man's life is nothing but an extended trek though the detours of art to recapture those one or two moments when his heart first opened."

Reginald Dwayne Betts is a poet and lawyer. A 2021 MacArthur Fellow, he is the Executive Director of Freedom Reads, a not-for-profit organization that is radically transforming the access to literature in prisons through the installation of Freedom Libraries in prisons across the US.

Cody Bruce is a thirty-seven-year-old mother of two wonderful young men. She's been incarcerated for seven years, during which she has honed her natural skills as a poet. Her ability to put words to the emotion has helped her through this tough time away from her children.

Marina Bueno is currently a resident of a prison in Florida. She finds purpose in keeping as busy as humanly possible with classes, work, writing, art, and most importantly, family and friends, and puppies. Yes, puppies.

Marcelo Hernandez Castillo is the author of *Children of the Land: A Memoir*, *Cenzontle*, winner of the A. Poulin, Jr., and *Dulce*, winner of the Drinking Gourd Prize. He is a founding member of the Undocupoets, which eliminated citizenship requirements from all major poetry book prizes in the US. He was the first undocumented student to graduate from the Helen Zell Writers Program. He teaches at St. Mary's College and Ashland University.

Natalie Diaz is a Pulitzer Prize-winning Mojave American poet, language activist, former professional basketball player, and educator. She is enrolled in the Gila River Indian Community and identifies as Akimel O'odham. She is currently an Associate Professor at Arizona State University.

Tongo Eisen-Martin is the author of *Heaven Is All Goodbyes*, which was shortlisted for the Griffin International Poetry Prize, received the California Book Award for Poetry, an American Book Award, and a PEN Oakland Book Award. He is also the author of *someone's dead already*. His newest collection is *Blood on the Fog* from City Lights Pocket Poets Series.

Nikky Finney was born by the sea in South Carolina and raised during the Civil Rights, Black Power, and Black Arts Movements. She authored *On Wings Made of Gauze*; *Rice*; *The World Is Round*; and *Head Off & Split*, the 2011 National Book Award winner for Poetry; and most recently *Love Child's Hotbed of Occasional Poetry*. She is the John H. Bennett Jr. Chair in Creative Writing and Southern Letters and Carolina Distinguished Professor at the University of South Carolina in Columbia.

Kennedy A. Gisege is an accomplished visual artist, poet, and the author of *The Liturgy of Smell*. His work can be found in *AGNI*, *South Dakota Review*, *Territory: A Journal of Place*, among other journals. He's the coeditor of *American Precariat: Parables Of Exclusion*. Kennedy has written several books under the pen name Ken Amen.

Gustavo Guerra doesn't have an MFA, his teeth, or a release date. He does, however, have tattoos and a passion for poetry, for creating art out of the dehumanizing loneliness of incarceration. His work can be found in Columbia University's *Exchange 03*, FIU's Community Literacy Journal, *Don't Shake the Spoon*, and wherever submissions find their final rest after rejections. He is serving a natural life sentence in the state of Florida.

Vicki Hicks is an incarcerated published writer who enjoys Exchange for Change classes. She has been challenged to write different genres though her creative writing classes and is looking forward to life after incarceration.

Jessica Hill is an expert service dog trainer at Homestead Correctional. When not training dogs for New Horizons Service Dogs, she writes and creates beautiful visual art for everyone in her community. She is also studying business so that she can start her own airbrushing company.

Randall Horton is the recipient of the Gwendolyn Brooks Poetry Award, the Bea Gonzalez Poetry Award, the Great Lakes College Association New Writers Award for Creative Nonfiction, and a National Endowment of the Arts Fellowship in Literature. He is a former member of the experimental performance group Heroes Are Gang Leaders, which received an American Book Award in Oral Literature and their musical project, *The Baraka Sessions*, was named best vocal jazz album by NPR. Randall's latest collection of poetry *{#289-128}* is published by the University of Kentucky (2020) and received the American Book Award in 2021. His memoir, *Dead Weight: A Memoir in Essays,* is published by Northwestern University Press. Randall is also cofounder of Radical Reversal, a music project with an emphasis on justice equity through the investigation of sound. Randall is a Professor of English at the University of New Haven.

Sandra Jackson is a mother of four who has been locked up for eleven years. She lost one of the four children at the time she was locked up and still misses him today. She is hoping to one day heal.

Catherine LaFleur is a poet working with Exchange for Change, a nonprofit bringing writing and educational programming to prisons in South Florida. She is the current Incarcerated Poet Laureate of the Luis Angel Hernandez Poet Laureateship for O, Miami Poetry Foundation and Exchange for Change. She won the inaugural PEN America Bell Chevigny Award. In 2022, she was awarded a Dornsife prize from UCLA and in 2023 published the poem, "Mother of Beasts" in *Massachusetts Review*. Catherine is a frequent contributor to *Don't Shake the Spoon* and *Prisoner Express*. She is the author of the blog, Adventures in Camp Prisoney Land.

Ada Limón is the author of six books of poetry, including *The Carrying*, which won the National Book Critics Circle Award for Poetry. Her new book of poetry, *The Hurting Kind*, is out now from Milkweed Editions. She is the 24th Poet Laureate of the United States.

Sarah Lynn Maatsch is a Buddhist trans woman that believes play and silliness should never be lost. She has worked in such diverse industries as aerospace engineering, cyber security, interactive entertainment, and retail party supplies. She is currently working on a spiritual book about cosmology and a new interactive story world.

Christopher Malec is the Luis Angel Hernandez Poet Laureate. As a writer of poetry and law, he blends these two worlds together to paint a clearer picture of what social justice needs in America. His work has been featured in *Poetry* magazine, NPR, and elsewhere. Incarcerated since the age of nineteen, he's currently serving life without parole.

Eduardo "Echo" Martinez writes from within a place that provides no view. His pen is penicillin to the oppressed and a call to action against silence worse than violence. He served as the inaugural Luis Angel Hernandez Poet Laureate

(2019–2021). His work has appeared in *The Nation, Cuban Counterpoints, Scalawag, These Words Are Fugitives*, and PEN America's Break Out series. He's been heard on PBS, CBS, and NPR. A writer for PEN's inaugural writer's bureau, Echo was born and raised in Miami, FL, and has spent twenty-three years incarcerated, still fighting for freedom, his ink being his greatest weapon.

John Murillo is author of the poetry collections *Up Jump the Boogie* and *Kontemporary Amerikan Poetry*. His honors include the Kingsley Tufts Poetry Award, the Poetry Society of Virginia's North American Book Award, the Four Quartets Prize from T. S. Eliot Foundation and the Poetry Society of America, and the Lucille Clifton Legacy Award from St. Mary's College of Maryland. His translation Rafael Alberti's *Concerning the Angels* is forthcoming from Four Way Books. He is professor of English and teaches in the MFA program at Hunter College.

Kenneth Nadeau is currently incarcerated. Poetry has given him purpose in a jungle of concrete. Poetry is his best friend. It listens to him. Soothes his broken heart. Wails by his side. Protects him from a lifetime of bad memories.

Angel Nafis is the author of *BlackGirl Mansion*. She is a Cave Canem fellow, the recipient of the Ruth Lilly and Dorothy Sargent Rosenberg Poetry Fellowship, a Creative Writing fellowship from the NEA, and a Jerome Hill Artist Fellowship. She teaches at the low-residency MFA program at Randolph College.

Leeann Parker is a 40-year-old, ex-gang member that has changed her life for the better. She is also a mother, who has longed for the chance to watch her children grow after almost twenty years. She is about to be released to start her Journey called life, and she is ready for it to begin.

James Pearl I am Afro American, 65-years-old. I started writing poetry in 2019 after attending a poetry class here at Everglades C.I. taught by Mr. George Franklin. Prior to that I had never written a poem. I always knew that there was something inside of me that I wanted to share with others. I had no idea how to do it until I started to take the Exchange For Change classes. I am now able to share with the world through images and expressions from voice within.

Christina Pernini loves to read, like, *loves* to read! When not working at the Pride Optical Laboratory in Homestead Correctional, becoming an expert eyeglass maker, she can be found on her bunk finishing another book.

Roque Raquel Salas Rivera is a Puerto Rican poet, editor, and translator of trans experience whose honors include being named Poet Laureate of Philadelphia, the Premio Nuevas Voces, the Ambroggio Prize, and a Lambda Literary Award. He lives, teaches, and writes in Puerto Rico and is currently working on the trans epic poem *Algarabía*, which will be published in 2025 by Graywolf Press.

Patrick Rosal is an interdisciplinary artist and author of five full-length poetry collections including *The Last Thing: New and Selected Poems*, which was named a best book of 2021 in the *Boston Globe*, and winner of the Poetry Society of America's William Carlos Williams Book Award. He is a fellow of John Simon Guggenheim Foundation, the National Endowment for the Arts, Fulbright Research Scholar program, and New Jersey School Counselor Association. He co-Directs the Institute for the Study of Global Racial Justice at Rutgers-Camden, where he is a Professor of English.

Nicole Sealey is the author of *The Ferguson Report: An Erasure*, winner of the 2024 OCM Bocas Prize for Poetry and a finalist for the NAACP Image Award in Poetry, and an excerpt from which was awarded the Forward Prize for Best Single Poem. She is also the author of *Ordinary Beast* and *The Animal After Whom Other Animals Are Named*, winner of the Drinking Gourd Chapbook Poetry Prize.

SHE>i is a self-proclaimed jill-of-all-writes from St. Thomas, U.S.V.I. The newly renamed author writes novels, screenplays, and songs. Though her formal background is in construction, her first love is the written word. SHE>i is one of four business names the author utilizes to protect her creative freedom and be unhindered by her past. Nor does SHE>i wish to let her past define her work. This author hopes to contribute love in every form to the world, understanding the importance of knowing one's gift, but more importantly—overstanding the greater importance in sharing it.

Evie Shockley is a poet and scholar who thinks, creates, and writes with her eye on a Black feminist horizon. Her books of poetry include *suddenly we*, *semiautomatic*, and *the new black*. Her work has twice garnered the Hurston/Wright Legacy Award, was a finalist for the Pulitzer Prize, and appears internationally. Her honors include the Lannan Literary Award for Poetry and the Stephen Henderson Award, and her joys include participating in such communities as Cave Canem, Poets at the End of the World, & the Community of Writers. Shockley is the Zora Neale Hurston Distinguished Professor of English at Rutgers University.

Patricia Smith, winner of the 2021 Poetry Foundation Ruth Lilly Award for Lifetime Achievement, is the author of eight critically acclaimed poetry collections, including *Unshuttered*, *Incendiary Art*, and *Blood Dazzler*. Smith is a chancellor of the Academy of American Poets, a member of the American Academy of Arts and Sciences, a Guggenheim Fellow, a National Endowment for the Arts grantee, a Neustadt International Prize for Literature finalist, and a four-time National Poetry Slam champion. She is a professor of creative writing at Princeton.

Sin à Tes Souhaits, a Black poet, cultural critic, and multimedia artist from East Las Vegas, is the former Clark County Poet Laureate and a fellow of Art for Justice, the Carol C. Harter, Beverly Rogers Black Mountain Institute, *Believer Magazine, Los Angeles Review of Books*, and other institutions. His writing is featured in the *Sun, Believer, Gen*, the *Rumpus*, and elsewhere. Sin founded and directs ACI Creative, a media consulting firm that works with writers, presses, and literary projects.

Vanessa Angélica Villarreal is the author of *Beast Meridian* (Noemi Press, 2017), recipient of a 2019 Whiting Award, a Kate Tufts Discovery Award nomination, and winner of the John A. Robertson Award for Best First Book of Poetry from the Texas Institute of Letters. Her writing has appeared in The *New York Times, Harper's Bazaar, Oxford American, Poetry* magazine, and elsewhere. She is a 2021 National Endowment for the Arts Poetry Fellow and a doctoral candidate at the University of Southern California in Los Angeles, where she is working on a poetry and a nonfiction collection while raising her son.

Erica "Ewok" Walker was raised in the small town of Jupiter, FL. Her courageous daughter, Sage, keeps her inspired to fight for criminal justice and mass incarceration reform, LGBTQ+ and women's rights, advocacy and ending the pharmaceutical corporations opioid pandemic. Ewok is a talented muralist, who loves anime, graphic novels, alternative and indie music, and is currently writing and illustrating her own graphic novel.

Candace Williams is a poet and interdisciplinary artist. *I Am the Most Dangerous Thing* (Alice James Books, 2023) is their debut full-length poetry collection. Candace earned their Bachelor of Arts in Philosophy, Politics, and Economics (PPE) from Claremont McKenna College and Master of Arts in Education from Stanford University. They grew up in the Pacific Northwest and found love and poetry in Brooklyn, New York. Now, Candace lives and makes art in New England.

GRATITUDE

Thank you to Tucson community organizations for introducing the Poetry Center's Art for Justice Reading Series at the University of Arizona Poetry Center from 2018-2020.

Ojalá Systems (a collective), opening presentation for Randall Horton on November 15, 2018; On March 21, 2019, Juliana Piccillo, Yolanda Gómez, and Erin Whitfield from the Tucson Sex Workers Outreach Project opened the presentation for Evie Shockley and Patrick Rosal; Grace Gámez, Deborah North, Nate McKowen, and Joe Watson representing the American Friends Service Committee, opening presentation for Nikky Finney on February 7, 2019; On April 4, 2019, Leah Bishop and Nadia Comaduran of the Florence Immigrant and Refugee Rights Project opened the presentation for Natalie Diaz; On September 26, 2019, Leilani Clark, representing BIPOC UNITED TUCSON, gave the opening presentation for Angel Nafis and Patricia Smith; On October 17, 2019, Timoteio Padilla, representing Sustainable Nations, gave the opening presentation for Tongo Eisen-Martin; and Lola Rainey, Tucson Bail Fund representative, gave the opening presentation for Ada Limón on February 20, 2020.

I would like to express my deepest gratitude to the Art for Justice Fund, Ford Foundation, and Rockefeller Philanthropy Advisors for their unwavering support. I am immensely thankful to Reginald Dwayne Betts, Joe Watson, Marcus Bullock, and Flikshop, as well as the dedicated University of Arizona Poetry Center Team and Triangle House Literary agency. A special acknowledgment goes to Maya Marshall, a gifted poet and editor, for her belief in this project and her thoughtful stewardship of this book. Maya, your support has been invaluable.

I am deeply grateful to my agent and champion, Kima Jones of Triangle House Literary, who empowered me with the vision, courage, and space to dream expansively for this book. Her unwavering support reminds me of the transformative power that emerges when Brown communities unite, lifting one another toward boundless possibility.

Thank you to all the poets who participated in such an important project. This book stands as a testament to the cumulative power of your work.

Lastly, I extend my heartfelt thanks to my writing community, who supported me as I worked tirelessly on this book while juggling a full-time job and the demands of the world: Emily Hockaday, John Espinoza, Jennifer Ortega, Jackie Sherbow, Justin Petropoulos, T.C. Tolbert, Open City Writers Group, Amanda Pennelly, Monica Wendel, Felicia Zamora and Matthew Zapruder, your unwavering support has made all the difference.

ABOUT HAYMARKET BOOKS

Haymarket Books is a radical, independent, nonprofit book publisher based in Chicago. Our mission is to publish books that contribute to struggles for social and economic justice. We strive to make our books a vibrant and organic part of social movements and the education and development of a critical, engaged, and internationalist Left.

We take inspiration and courage from our namesakes, the Haymarket Martyrs, who gave their lives fighting for a better world. Their 1886 struggle for the eight-hour day—which gave us May Day, the international workers' holiday—reminds workers around the world that ordinary people can organize and struggle for their own liberation. These struggles—against oppression, exploitation, environmental devastation, and war—continue today across the globe.

Since our founding in 2001, Haymarket has published more than nine hundred titles. Radically independent, we seek to drive a wedge into the risk-averse world of corporate book publishing. Our authors include Angela Y. Davis, Arundhati Roy, Keeanga-Yamahtta Taylor, Eve Ewing, Aja Monet, Mariame Kaba, Naomi Klein, Rebecca Solnit, Olúfẹ́mi O. Táíwò, Mohammed El-Kurd, José Olivarez, Noam Chomsky, Winona LaDuke, Robyn Maynard, Leanne Betasamosake Simpson, Howard Zinn, Mike Davis, Marc Lamont Hill, Dave Zirin, Astra Taylor, and Amy Goodman, among many other leading writers of our time. We are also the trade publishers of the acclaimed Historical Materialism Book Series.

Haymarket also manages a vibrant community organizing and event space in Chicago, Haymarket House, the popular Haymarket Books Live event series and podcast, and the annual Socialism Conference.

ABOUT THE EDITOR

Diana Marie Delgado is a poet, editor, playwright, and the author of *Tracing the Horse* and *Late-Night Talks with Men I Think I Trust*. With extensive experience in executive leadership, Delgado is committed to uplifting writers and cultivating vibrant creative communities. She holds degrees from UC Riverside and Columbia University's MFA program in poetry and resides in Tucson, Arizona.